Acting on Impulse

Acting on Impulse
The Art of Making Improv Theater

Carol Hazenfield

Coventry Creek Press
Berkeley, California

ACTING ON IMPULSE
Coventry Creek Press/October 2002

All Rights Reserved
Copyright © 2002 by Carol Hazenfield

Book and cover design by Tony Lijphart
Back cover photo by Derrick Dobbs

No part of this book may be reproduced or transmitted in any form or by any means, electronic or mechanical, including photocopying, recording, or by any information storage and retrieval system, without written permission from the author, except for the inclusion of brief quotations in a review.

Adaptation from *The Empty Space* by Peter Brook
used by permission of the author.
Excerpt from "States of Reading" copyright 1999 by Sven Birkerts
reprinted from *Readings* with the permission of
Graywolf Press, Saint Paul, Minnesota.

Coventry Creek Press
P.O. Box 7160
Berkeley, CA 94707-0160

Printed in the United States of America

Library of Congress Control Number: 2002091073
Paperback ISBN-10: 0-9719112-3-1
ISBN-13: 978-0-9719112-3-9

First Edition
Second Printing

For my parents

Contents

Acknowledgments

Introduction

Part One: Process

    1 **Raising the Curtain**—Improv as Theater   9
    2 **Being Caught Off-Guard**—The Fundamentals   17
    3 **Escaping the Brain**—Going Back to Your Body   27
    4 **Getting Got**—Revealing Emotion   37
    5 **Pushing Your Partner**—Improv Etiquette   45
    6 **Long Time No Talk**—Making Magic in Silence   55
    7 **The Truth Right Now**—Stimulus/Response Cycles   67
    8 **Finding the Shiny Thing**—Seeking Pleasure   83

Part Two: Nuts and Bolts

    9 **Whose Journey Is It?**—Protagonist-Centered Storytelling   91
    10 **Playing with Fire**—Creating Richer Characters   113
    11 **Acting Like a Human**—Objectives and Tactics   131
    12 **The How and Why of Where**—Creating Environments   141
    13 **Get Off My Foot**—Group Scenes   163
    14 **It Ain't Just Window Dressing**—The Essence of Genres   171
    15 **Looking into the Abyss**—Long Forms   179
    16 **Improv Surgery**—How to Fix a Broken Scene   191
    17 **An Improvised Path**—The Artist's Journey   197

Appendices

    A **Ideas for Teachers**   209
    B **Exercise Materials**   229

Index of Exercises   234

Acknowledgments

Many thanks to all my colleagues and friends at Bay Area Theatresports™ (BATS) in San Francisco, where I received my first improv training and had my eyes opened to the possibilities of the form. Through BATS, I was privileged to work with great improvisers from all over the world; they taught me a lot, shook up my thinking, and provided companionship, fun, and some hearty discussions along the way.

Thanks to Keith Johnstone for creating Theatresports and for the fascinating theories he has developed.

My first improv teacher, Rafe Chase, was my mentor for performing and teaching. His kindness, enthusiasm, and creation of new ideas have been consistently inspirational. To Rebecca Stockley, Dean of the School of BATS, I owe a debt of gratitude. She is a magic gardener who discovers and grows teachers. I'm also indebted to Creative Advantage and the Fratelli Bologna for giving me the opportunity to teach improv extensively in the business community.

This project started life as a twelve-page handout written for a narrative class. That it grew up to be a book is due in large part to the following people:

Doug Nunn, who read the very first draft and lavished praise and enthusiasm on me; Cort Worthington, who generously read the second draft with an editorial eye and gave invaluable advice; Chris Miller, who provided support for the ideas and the writing when I was ready to chuck the whole thing; Ann Swanberg, who not only read an early draft, but also spent many hours discussing improv with me as we shared our hopes for what improv could become; Kirk Livingston, whose boundless support, encouragement, and input got me through many stalled episodes and whose own work provided the springboard for several ideas in the book; Lauren Artress, who keeps me on track in writing and in life; Reed Kirk Rahlmann, who offered practical advice at critical junctures; Caroline Pincus, my editor, who helped develop the manuscript; and Annelise Zamula, who provided hawk-eyed proofreading skills.

To all the students who participated in my classes at BATS and Living Improv: it was a joy throughout. You made it OK for me to experiment and grow. Thanks, too, for your hearty embrace of a new way of improvising, and for your amazing ability to challenge yourselves and me.

Thank you to family and friends, who didn't even know exactly what I was up to, but who were sure on principle that it was worth doing. They buoyed my spirits during the long process of writing.

Lastly, to my husband, Tony: thank you for your beautiful design work and your unflagging support. Your confidence and love make everything possible.

A note about the exercises:

The origin of many improv games and acting exercises is unknown, as theater training is an oral tradition with creative iterations along the way. Some of the exercises in this book were developed by me over the course of the past several years and were no doubt influenced by the many teachers I had when I was an acting and improv student. Many exercises were created or handed down by others. Wherever possible I have cited the originators of exercises. I apologize in advance for any omissions or errors.

Introduction

For as long as I can remember, people have been telling me that I don't understand how things work in the *real world*. And for about thirty years I bought in, big time. I believed I was missing the point that everyone else so clearly grasped: that the real world is a concrete and finite place, with a long list of rules carved into the bedrock.

Then one day, BLAMMO! I figured out that there *is* no real world. It's all a matter of angles. The world is what we each see from our individual perch. That old notion of the real world is just a construct that supports the status quo—it's a boogeyman conjured up to scare us into keeping quiet and copying the guy sitting next to us.

The world exists as we create it. You and I haven't stumbled onto a rigid stage set, with our lines and actions predetermined at the moment of our births; we are fluid, inquisitive creatures who can shape the world to our liking.

I had this epiphany in my first improv class, where I was minding my own business, trying to learn a new acting form. As happens to a lot of people, improv changed the way I felt about everything. The improvisers I met were joyful, flawed, funny and mischievous, and I understood for the first time that the old crabby guys were wrong. Improv smashed all the rocks, raining pebbles on the rules.

I had performed for years in scripted theater, but improvising was so exciting I often felt drunk. I staggered around this new terrain, boggled by its immensity; it seemed a world without boundaries.

So it was surprising to smack into some. It turns out there's a "real world" mentality about improv, too. The conventional wisdom is that improv audiences are looking for a quick comic payoff, that there isn't time to do more meaningful work. As a result, most improv performances are game-centered and are played fast and funny. Much of the humor is derived from seeing people in ridiculous situations (he's naked at a job interview, her hair is on fire) and from watching characters squirm and twist and survive the experience.

It reminds me of Australia. You know how it's all developed around the edges, while the Outback is wide open and barely inhabited? That's how improv feels. We've settled the game-and-wacky-comedy region pretty successfully. We have maps of this territory. But what's going on in the Outback?

This question led me to look at improv from a new perspective. I loved teaching and performing, but I missed the substantial nature of scripted work and I wondered if it would be possible to create improv with the richness and depth of traditional theater. I also wondered if working in a new way could help us know ourselves on a deeper level. So I started experimenting with my classes. The focus of our work was on good acting, connection, and textured storytelling. We practiced the skills and mounted shows. We discovered that scenes with depth of character and relationships excited improvisers and audiences alike.

Working this way means improvising from the heart. And that calls for a new kind of training. Traditional improv classes focus quite a bit on mental skills: how to empty your mind and be more flexible in your thinking. *Acting on Impulse* emphasizes listening to your inner life, following your body, and reacting emotionally as well as verbally.

When we're improvising from the heart, the entertainment comes from the interaction among the players. Interactive improv can be as surprising, delightful, and funny as game-prov, with the added benefit that the stories emerge from the relationships and the narrative grows organically. Wonderfully comic scenes can be created this way.

And, bonus of bonuses—we can do dramatic improvisation. Once players have the skills and courage to go into more dangerous territory, we can take the audience on a ride through all aspects of the human experience—not just the comic parts. In one of our shows, we had a taut, dramatic scene involving an adult brother and sister. They had a troubled relationship, and as the scene unfolded, the brother had to ask the sister to donate a kidney to save his life. The sister said no.

Yowzers! You could feel the shock and excitement in the audience. They sensed the danger and so did the improvisers. It's this exploration of the unexpected territory, both internal and external, that appeals to me. *Acting on Impulse* was created as a path into *that* real world, and this book is a map for your travels.

Acting on Impulse aims to create theater alive with commitment and risk. It's for improvisers, actors, teachers, and students who are already familiar with the basics of improv. While the focus is on improv as a performance medium, scripted actors will benefit too, as you learn to listen with your whole self, respond from your gut instincts and create emotional depth in your characters.

The first time through, it's best to read and use the book in the order in which it's written; each chapter builds on the one before, and many of the exercises make more sense if you've done the previous ones. And hey—you've got to actually *do* the exercises to get the most from them. In certain cases, I suggest you do the exercise before reading any further, as some are so experiential they defy deconstruction until you've done them yourself. Most of the exercises are intended for groups. It works best if you have a leader to direct them.

That's all you need to know for now. See you in the Outback.

Carol Hazenfield
April 2002

Part One

Process

Raising the Curtain
Improv as Theater

When the audience settle into their seats at a scripted play, they expect to see good acting, relationships with depth, emotional commitment, and rich characterizations. Their standards are gloriously high.

At an improv show, they expect to laugh, go home, and forget about it.

Why do improvisers settle for that? Why do we play it so safe?

When actors are courageous enough to fulfill subconscious desires—our own, and those of the audience—improv can actually be the most dangerous, exciting form of theater. No written play can match the edge and spontaneity of an improv show—the audience members know they're watching the actors' imaginations at work. The promise of unintended revelation adds an exciting note of voyeurism to the proceedings. If people are going to watch us through keyholes, let's give them something worth watching. Let's make the show three-dimensional.

Some players might say, "What's wrong with improv the way it is? We make people laugh and we're being spontaneous." That's great. *But is that all there is?* Yes, we can get on stage, act silly and call it a day. Chickens can dance with their heads cut off, but it ain't exactly ballet. With few exceptions, improv shows resemble ersatz situation comedies, consisting of plastic sketches with cardboard characters. Improvisers work overtime to look cool and unfazed when something unexpected happens on stage, adopting poses of ironic distance to shield themselves from risk. It's no wonder improv is the poor relation to theater. We're not challenging each other or the audience.

Let's say you're watching the play *Fool for Love* by Sam Shepard. As you are drawn deeper into the story of Eddie and May, you might begin to recognize (almost against your will) aspects of your own life. If the actors are engaging and courageous, you may feel you're watching a slow-motion car accident, unable to look away. The more troubled their relationship becomes, the more you long for a resolution, for redemption. It almost hurts to watch the play.

Or, let's say you're watching Christopher Durang's comedy *The Actor's Nightmare*. You laugh from the safety of your theater seat at the struggles of George Spelvin, the Everyman who finds himself cast in a play he doesn't know. The worse his predicament, the more you laugh. As you begin to understand his character, you look forward with glee to the next stage of the nightmare.

"But those are plays!" you say. "We can't expect to match the wit of Durang or the bite of Shepard!" Yes, we can! I'll grant you that we will probably never use words as cleverly or efficiently as these writers do. But we can create the same levels of comedy, tension, sorrow, and joy. *Because* we're improvising, the stakes are higher—there's no script to act as a safety net. If one character challenges another to a duel, neither actor knows who's going to be alive at the end. *That* creates dramatic tension or comic delight. If we're willing to truly take the plunge into not-knowingness we can draw out deeper performances from each other. We can create character-driven comedy and dramatic improvisation—even tragedy. It's perfectly possible to tell stories of sacrifice, growth, love, and hate, in addition to stories of pure fancy. We just haven't been asking ourselves to do it.

The predominant thinking is that we should give the audience what they want. The trouble is, audiences want what they've seen before. They want what they know. We can either follow our audience or lead them. I vote for leading.

I believe improv can be art. But it doesn't come cheaply. Compelling improvised theater requires strong acting skills and a deep understanding of character, relationship, and narrative. You'll need new skills and a willingness to expand your thinking about what improv can be.

By expecting more of ourselves as actors, we can fulfill improv's deeper promises: raw human stories with edges and twists, actors who are buffeted by unexpected events. If we make the audience laugh, let's have the laughs come from the recognition of human frailties and idiosyncrasies. Let's make our audiences angry, make them cry—push the boundaries and then cross them. Let's frighten the bejeezus out of them.

Sound good? Sound scary? OK, so how do we gather the courage to do that? Make no mistake, this is a risky business: we'll be connecting with and revealing our innermost desires and fears. We'll be re-imagining ourselves and reclaiming the power of improvisation to move and enchant an audience. We'll open ourselves up to joy and heartache by interacting with our colleagues as people, not just performers. Improvising from the heart leaves no room for playing it safe.

First we'll look at the foundational elements of good improv. I'll then guide you through exercises to connect with yourself on a deeper, more primitive level—through your body and emotions. Then you'll practice acting on your impulses with fellow players. Lastly, in "Nuts and Bolts," you'll find ideas for creating better scenes and stories, as well as solutions for common improv problems.

This journey requires attention and practice; powerful spontaneous theater is created through commitment, experimentation, and risk.

NOTES ON HOW TO WORK

Most improv training uses the "outside-in" model: follow these rules, behave in this way, and these results will occur. Here we'll be looking at how to improvise from the *inside out*. Working this way is experiential, and is based on behaving truthfully in any given situation. You'll learn to follow your impulses as they occur, without filtering them through a set of improv rules or games. When you improvise instinctually, from your own unique experience, you can be effective in *every* scene. And you'll have 'way more fun than when you were worrying about all the rules.

Improvising truthfully is a multi-layered process. Improvisers almost universally report that it's hard to separate out their real-life strengths and limitations from those they experience on stage. For example, an improviser I know smiles constantly, even when she doesn't feel like it. She knows it's false, and yet her lips keep curling up. Which is fine, unless she's playing a villain, and then she just looks silly. Other people, who have always relied on logic, find themselves frustrated when they improvise. Their partners in scenes often act illogically (i.e., spontaneously) and these folks are at a loss to respond. No doubt the same problem arises in real life. Whether we like it or not, improvising holds up a clear and unerring mirror and challenges us to look at ourselves.

But guess what? We also get to discover and exercise the underused parts of ourselves: logical types get to stretch their emotional wings, the smilers get to frown and act nasty—everybody wins. Improvising opens channels we didn't even know we had: channels of perception, communication, and emotion. Keeping these pipes open is a tall order; it means we'll be asking ourselves to operate in a completely new way so we can create theater that excites and challenges. Here are some suggestions to get you started in the right direction.

The Conscious Mind

In any given class, there are always some smart students for whom improv comes very hard. Smart students think that if they *understand* enough, they will be good improvisers. They think that if they take enough notes, ask enough questions, and learn the rules, they will succeed. It usually doesn't work that way. In fact, I've noticed that the most effective improvisers are often the people who don't care about the rules, who experiment endlessly. These players listen to their experience and don't get knotted up thinking there's a "right" way to improvise.

Your brain is not as smart as you think it is. When it comes to improvising, your brain will get in the way more often than it will help.

Your brain is not as smart as you think it is. When it comes to improvising, your brain will get in the way more often than it will help. Improv is a *process* and it has to seep into you; you can't willfully decide to become a good improviser. You can only practice. When you've practiced long enough, you should start to notice improvements.

Is there a good use of the conscious mind in improv? Sure. Use your conscious mind to take in information. Use it to help you stay physically safe on stage, to read books, to listen to your teachers. Other than that, SHUT IT DOWN. Shut it down while you're improvising and keep it quiet right after scenes. The experience you have during an interaction is far more important, and more real, than your analysis of it. The first process is the act of *being*, and it involves your whole self; the second is the act of *thinking* and involves only your mind. If you're exploring brand-new territory, your mind may rebel and attempt to fit new experiences into old definitions. That's one of its jobs, after all—to process experience and look for patterns. You can't do much about that, but you *can* listen to your body and heart first and encourage your mind to hang back a bit.

Changing Habits

If you're trying to change an improv habit, it's next door to useless to say "Stop doing that." Instead, you need to call upon the laws of physics and replace the old action with a new one. Let's say you want to stop driving in scenes. ("Driving" means you control things by talking too much.) It's usually not effective to say to yourself right before a scene, "don't drive this time." Since you're comfortable driving, that command is counterintuitive, and it will almost always fail. And anyway, it's just your brain talking.

Choose something to do instead of driving, such as connecting with your partner's eyes, or making physical offers.[1] These actions take up positive space ("don't drive" occupies negative space; it's the absence of action). If you choose a new activity that doesn't come easily to you, you will expend a lot of focus and energy on that new activity and won't have any left over for driving. With practice you'll find the old habit has dropped away. When choosing a new activity, pick something you've wanted to work on anyway; that way, you'll get a double benefit.

---

1. An offer is anything you say or do on stage that defines an aspect of the scene.

When you're trying to grow your work, focus on one thing at a time. Give yourself one point of concentration, not ten.

Concentration

I've noticed two kinds of concentration. There's the coiled snake, bug-eyed, tensed-up "I'M CONCENTRATING!" kind of concentration that you often see when improvisers are warming up or watching a scene, terrified that they'll miss something. Then there's the sort of Buddhist concentration, which is relaxed and attentive, and operates like a sieve, letting wayward thoughts flow through. The big, important chunks stay in the sieve; the small, unimportant bits of silt fall out the bottom.

I definitely recommend the Buddhist over the snake. Trust that the sieve will retain the big, important pieces you need and relinquish the small, unimportant ones. A lot of the work ahead of you involves letting go and getting out of your own way. Quiet, relaxed attention will coax out the real, passionate you that's hiding under all the noise and effort.

Record Keeping

Some improvisers take tons of notes. They transcribe verbatim everything the teacher says. Others never write anything down. I suggest you split the difference and keep an improv journal. For one thing, it keeps your conscious mind occupied and makes it feel useful. It's also a great way to record your experiences and tendencies. For instance, if, after a scene, you realize that you blocked[2] (yet again), you might make a note of what was going on in the scene when you blocked. After awhile you might see a pattern forming. For example, you may discover that you only block when someone tries to lower your status[3] on stage; that's a handy thing to know.

Writing down little odd notions you don't even quite understand is also useful, as it affirms your internal process in an outward way. Let's say you're watching a scene, and afterward

---

2. To "block" is to deny the reality of the scene.

3. The idea of status behaviors was created by Keith Johnstone and is discussed in his books *Impro* and *Impro for Storytellers*. Status work is magical. Learn it and be transformed.

the thought comes to you, "Fish scenes promote emotionally high stakes." That sounds truly weird, right? Put it down anyway. If nothing else, it will make your journal more interesting to read later. And who knows? You may be exactly right about fish scenes.

If note taking interferes with your ability to *experience* scenes, lose the notebook. When you're watching improv, you can do it as an invested participant or an observer. Choose investment. Let improv affect you. Wait until a scene or exercise is finished to make notes.

I have several students who will grab their pens and scribble away between scenes; it's obvious that something has struck their fancy, and they want to capture it for themselves. That's the ticket.

This is *your* ride—everything that follows is essentially one gigantic suggestion for how to tap into and express your internal world. My advice? Bring a flashlight.

Notes

Being Caught Off-Guard
The Fundamentals

To play truthfully on stage, you must follow your instincts as fully as possible. And those instincts are inextricably entwined with your *self*—your personality, your body, your family, and little bits of every experience you ever had. If you started improvising in the hope of hiding yourself from the world, I've got some bad news for you. You'll never reach your full potential as a performer. Instead, you should cleave to the self as the only basis for truthful improvising. Not until you can reveal your own inner life can you hope to create fictional characters with dimension and depth. Your inner workings can be quick, shifty little things. Coaxing them out of hiding requires you to make space and shut up. When you do speak, you must be honest. In prettier language: *slow down, simplify,* and *speak the truth.*

SLOW DOWN

An improv stage is often a whirling vortex of waving arms and shouting mouths. It's hard not to get sucked in. We have a lot to keep track of and our adrenaline is pumping. We need to slow down so we can feel what's happening to us and respond to it.

Slow down, simplify, and speak the truth.

Imagine your chest is made of metal (like the Tin Woodman in *The Wizard of Oz*) fitted with double doors that swing open to reveal the inner workings of your heart. When you take time to be genuinely affected in a scene, those doors can operate and we get a glimpse *inside* the character.

Physical Stillness

Even improvisers who have learned to move economically on stage will often dilute the power of their work with small, random movements as they wriggle out of emotion's grasp. The only way to work in concert with your body is from a place of stillness. Genuine stillness.

Moving away from emotion is a means of staying on guard and in control—of the moment, the scene, and the relationship. If we can stand still when we have the urge to run, if we can *stay* off-balance, our scenes will be riskier and stronger. It takes courage to be still when we are caught off-guard by emotion. But being caught off-guard is the essence of theater. The simple act of being still can channel your impulses and emotions into a powerful wave that will erupt out of you. Let yourself be swept away. Learn to plant your feet. When you're standing still, do it without rocking from side to side. When you move, move with purpose—to get somewhere, to get away from something, or to act on your objectives.

Being caught off-guard is the essence of theater.

Verbal Stillness

In addition to physical stillness, we must cultivate verbal stillness as well. Most improvisers talk too much. We find the longest way to say even the simplest thing. If you're chatty, a good rule of thumb is talk about one-fifth as much as you think you need to. Show, don't tell. This will unclutter your stage life tremendously. We improvisers often announce what we're going to do instead of just doing it: "I'm leaving now/I'm getting a drink/I'm looking for those papers you asked for, Mr. Hodges." It's always better simply to *leave*, to *drink*, to *look*. It's not necessary to do a play-by-play. Let's assume the audience will recognize a person drinking no matter how bad the mime.

Talk about one-fifth as much as you think you need to.

When we *do* instead of *talk*, we open the possibility that our actions will have an effect on us and we can move deeper into the character. For instance: Let's say in a scene, I'm looking through my dead father's desk for his will. I move with purpose, intent on discovering what he left to me. If I perform this act silently, I have a good chance of having an emotional response when I find the will. If I talk, my chances plummet. This principle also goes for emotional offers: "You're really making me angry/I love you/I'm afraid," etc. It's much more powerful to *show* these emotions than to talk about them.

Improvisers also have a tendency to ask one question, then another, then another, and their poor partners have yet to answer the first one. I believe this often happens because the first question was emotionally risky, such as, "Don't you love me?" Which is often followed up by something like "Don't I make enough money for you? Is it the way I dress?" These additional questions dilute the danger and power of the first, "Don't you love me?"

The other improviser in this scene doesn't know which question to answer, and will often choose to answer the last question they heard, which was the weakest ("Is it the way I dress?") Now, instead of a scene about love on the rocks, we've got a scene about a fashion dispute. Safe and *dull*.

When you ask a question, wait for the answer. Incorporating this one idea alone will radically change your interactions. Remember that you *need to hear* the answer. After you've asked a question, it's your partner's turn to talk.

Some improv offers need a bubble of silence around them to underscore their importance. When you or your partner makes a big offer, let it hang and shimmer in the air for a moment. Let the audience hold its breath as you feel the tension rise between you and your partner. Then when you speak—KA-POW!

Like the rests in music, silence gives shape and meaning to our words. Think about the opening notes of Beethoven's Fifth Symphony: da-da-da-DUM. (*Silence.*) Da-da-da-DUM. If you remove the silence, you've got a much weaker piece of music.

Trust silence. Often, the most moving moments on stage have no words at all.

> DO instead of TALK, and you open the possibility that your actions will have an effect on you.

> When you ask a question, wait for the answer.

Simplify

To create the texture and depth of scripted theater we don't need to make things more complex. Simple, beefy offers create the opportunity for strong emotional responses. Improvising simply is often more difficult than slowing down, because we all seem to think complexity is better. It isn't. It *really* isn't in improv. Some techniques for simplifying are:

- use the simplest possible language
- play your objective
- make the strongest choice

Use Simple Language

The more complicated the scene, the more trouble you're in from the get-go. Complicated scenes usually require players to work only from their heads, making it impossible to inhabit their bodies or emotions.

Keep things open. Make room for emotion. A clear, simple offer is much easier for your partner to respond to than some fancy, around-the-park-and-back-again idea. Here's an example I see all the time in class:

Wife: Hi, Sweetie. [*Said in a listless tone*]

Husband: Is something wrong, honey?

Wife: I think so. I can't help noticing that you seem lately like you have something you want to do or say, but I can't tell what it is, and it's difficult for me to know what my response should be. I find you're being very passive-aggressive lately. I don't have the faintest idea how to communicate with you. [*etc., etc., etc.*]

Husband: What?

The poor husband doesn't know how to respond because the wife is being too complicated. A simpler version might be:

Wife: Hi, Sweetie. [*Said in a listless tone*]

Husband: Is something wrong, honey?
Wife: I don't think you love me anymore.

Now the husband has something to work with, and the wife can relax and not talk so much—it's not going to be her turn again for awhile.

One more way to simplify language: When asked a yes-or-no question, answer with "yes" or "no." This not only simplifies scenes, it galvanizes them and moves the action forward. Here's an example where Player B is equivocating:

Player A: Are you going to kill me?
Player B: That depends. *[Player A doesn't have any emotional response yet, because this offer doesn't generate one.]*
A: On what?
B: On whether or not you give me the jewels. *[At this point, it will still be difficult for Player A to have a response, because we have avoided the danger by putting conditions on death. Player A may start bargaining to keep the jewels.]*
A: What if I told you where Hermione was instead? *[Hermione WHO?]*

Let's play that scene again, using the yes-or-no idea.

A: Are you going to kill me?
B: Yes. *[Now Player A has something to work with!]*
A: *[Fearfully]* I don't want to die! *[Player A is now begging for his life. Much more fun for all concerned.]*

Now the scene can move forward. We don't have to watch a tap dance before getting to the crux of the matter. Remember, your goal should be to play with strength and truthfulness. Bold offers create more emotional possibilities than non-specific, drawn-out offers. Say yes or no.

When asked a yes-or-no question, answer with "yes" or "no."

One more thing about the yes-or-no approach. It gets a strong response from the audience. I believe that's because in life, we often mince words. It's startling and refreshing to hear someone say yes or no and *nothing else*.

Play Your Objective

In real life, we know what we want and we take action to get it. If you have any doubts about this, watch children working their parents in the toy aisle of the grocery store. They try as many tactics as necessary to get what they want and they don't stop until they get the toy, or until they understand that they cannot win. This energized and single-minded activity is called pursuing an objective.

Objectives are standard issue for acting in traditional theater, and woefully absent from improv. They're so important, in fact, that I devote an entire chapter to them later on (chapter 11); for now, here's an overview: if your character's objective is to get love, play that as clearly as possible. Make all your offers (verbal and non-verbal) work toward that goal. You may try seduction, bullying, pity, charm, or any number of tactics, but make sure that everything you do serves the objective of getting love. This not only simplifies the scene for you and your partner, it's a gift to the audience as well. It gives them something to root for, an investment in the scene.

> *In real life, we know what we want and we take action to get it.*

Make Strong Choices

If it were easy to make risky choices, everybody would be an astronaut and nobody would go into accounting. The same fear that pulls us away from risk in life pushes us toward weak choices on stage:

> *If it were easy to make risky choices, everybody would be an astronaut, and nobody would go into accounting.*

Player A: Suzie, I have some bad news for you.
B: Is it about my kitty?
A: Yes. I'm afraid it's sick.

This kitty will invariably get well again, and the scene will be weak. Not only is the cat merely sick, it's *invisible*. If the kitty were dead (with no hope of resuscitation), the scene would be stronger because the stakes would be higher. The scene would be even better if there was no cat at all, and the interaction was between the two women directly.

Work toward making all your choices strong choices. Here's a list of some common weak choices, and their stronger siblings:

Weak Choice	Strong Choice
I like you	I love you
I dislike you	I hate you
I'm frustrated	I'm angry
I misplaced it	I broke it
You're on probation	You're fired

Making the strongest choice takes practice. Set aside some time with your ensemble or class to play short scenes. The players watching the scene can call out "stronger choice" when an adjustment is needed.

Speak the Truth

Often an improviser will speak the character's *words*, but will not support those words with integrated emotions or physicality. So you may have a scene where one improviser says to another: "I really love you," but nothing in the actor's manner, tone, or face makes us believe it's true. Sometimes the improviser lacks basic acting skills, but I believe that more often it comes down to fear. (If you think you're noticing a motif here, you're right.) The words slip out before the actor can censor them, but the body clamps down and doesn't let the emotion out.

It's hard to be truthful about our inner lives (or those of the characters we play). But if we hope to be inhabited by our characters, to be expressive conduits for their hopes, dreams, and fears, we have to find a way to speak the truth in simple, direct language.

One way to practice is my Primal Truths exercise. The purpose of this exercise is two-fold: 1) to let players note how it feels when they're telling the truth about something important to them (and to note changes in their bodies and voices), and 2) to observe truth telling in others. This gives us an insight into what the audience feels when they see truthful behavior on stage.

If we hope to be inhabited by our characters, to be expressive conduits for their hopes, dreams, and fears, we must speak the truth in simple, direct language.

Primal Truths

The improvisers pair up and sit where they can talk quietly without being overheard. One improviser will be the speaker, the other the listener. The speaker will do all three rounds of the exercise. When he has finished, he will be the listener for his partner. Each improviser will be telling a story from his life that illustrates something that is true about him. True with a capital T. (Something meatier than "I wear a size 10 shoe.") It's helpful to pick something that you've been dealing with lately, perhaps an unresolved issue. Whatever you choose, it should be something you might be reluctant to tell a lot of people, but something you're willing to risk telling your partner in this setting. The information you share will remain between you and your partner.

The first recounting should be short, no more than one or two minutes in length. For instance, I may tell someone, "Ever since I stopped teaching to write this book, I'm alone a lot and I have a sense of having pushed off one shore, but not landed yet on the new shore. I know I'm a good teacher; I can feel the effect my work has on a class, but I don't know anything about myself as a writer. My ego's been taking a beating lately. I never realized how much ego-gratification I get from teaching. I don't know for sure where I'm headed, and sometimes I'm not even sure where I've been." (*This is round one.*)

In round two, I will pare down my words to state the same truth in one or two sentences, such as: "Lately, I've been having a bit of an identity crisis. I feel adrift, and being alone all the time is making it worse." In round three, I tell the same truth with as few words (as "primally") as possible: "I'm lost and it scares me."

With each round, I'm trying to get to the essential truth that's *underneath* all my words. I may be surprised by the primal truth once I get to it. During my part of the exercise, it's important that my partner listen without comment. When I have finished, I will listen to his story.

The exercise lets us experience truth telling from the inside and the outside. It affects people in different ways, but I've found it nearly always has a deep effect. Telling our truths opens us to others.

When I'm directing, if characters are being overly verbal and dancing around the underlying issue, I will tell the players to switch to Primal Truths (what's *underneath* what the character has been saying). This usually gets the scene moving in a more powerful direction.

When you're learning to speak the character's truth, trust your instincts. Improvisers' instincts are usually correct. The trick is to distinguish between a genuine instinct and a protective mechanism. For instance, a moment may come in a scene when the most truthful choice is for the character to be vulnerable (which the improviser may not want to do). The improviser may choose instead to get angry, then debate with me that that was where the *character* led them. I won't spend a lot of energy arguing the point. Instead, I'll ask them to do the moment again, and try vulnerability, and see how it feels. Usually the improviser can see which was the truer impulse, and which was just a fight-or-flight response.

Speaking the truth in real life requires that we *listen to ourselves* first, and then release our truth. The Primal Truths exercise can be done silently, internally. I was once in a conversation with my husband, in which he was telling me about a behavior of mine that was hurtful to him. As I listened, my first response was to feel defensive, and I could sense myself stockpiling excuses while he was talking. But then I breathed and remained still, and allowed my inner truth to come out, and it was very, very simple: "I'm scared." It wasn't at all the response I would have made a moment before, when my brain was full of defensive maneuvers and shouting about my innocence. But it was the simple truth, and the conversation took us to an unexpected and new understanding of one another.

The more you work with Primal Truths, the easier it will be to access them onstage and off.

The portal to fresh, vibrant improv swings open in those peculiar moments when we surprise ourselves, when we're off-balance and out of control. Seeking the out-of-balance condition

Speaking the truth requires that we listen to ourselves first, and then respond.

runs counter to our social training. But whether you know it or not, that's what you've signed up for. That's what theater is all about.

You have a choice when you improvise. You can walk onstage wearing your ironic overcoat and playing it safe, or you can enter the deep unknown willing to share yourself with the audience. If you choose the second path, your most able assistants will be silence, stillness, and simplicity. These three companions make it possible to feel your instincts stirring within you, and to act on those impulses with vigor.

Escaping the Brain
Going Back to Your Body

I am sixteen years old. The tent is dark, the night cold. Around me I can hear the deep, regular breathing of my friends. The pine trees brush against the wind as Jim's fingers fumble with the zippers of our sleeping bags. My world is warm and dizzy, all hands and lips as we shoot into the far reaches of first love. The hours are elastic, both endless and fleeting. No thinking or deciding NOW: I simply plunge into the next phase of my life, body first.

The first time I improvised I was back in that tent. I felt wild and free, like a centaur thundering through the woods.

And then I started to learn all the rules. Before long I was just a plain old bookworm again, improvising from the neck up. I was out of danger and living safely in my head.

I see this same phenomenon all the time among my colleagues and students. The more experienced we are, the worse it gets. Improv turns into an exercise in decision making. Time and again, I've watched scenes where I can see an improviser evaluating a situation, weighing the options and then choosing the next course of action. After clever scenes I've often heard players bragging along these lines: "I knew early on that we needed a funny policeman to bring back the diamond offer. I was waiting all through the scene for the right time to say it."

Well, OK. If that's the way you want to play. And you'll have plenty of company if you do, for many of us have reduced improvising to watching, deciding, and talking. But the further away we pull from our hearts and bodies, the deader our improv becomes.

Wanna be a centaur again? Wanna feel your leathery hooves pounding the peat? Some people think we have to trick ourselves into primitive behavior, because our social training is so strong it will always kick in unless we do an end run around it. I don't believe that. We don't have to trick our minds; we have to unleash our bodies. Thundering through the woods is addictive. When you do it once, you want to do it again.

I'm not saying it's not scary. It's thrilling, like driving too fast with the top down. Centaurs are naked and powerful. They like sex. They're nasty. They crave pleasure.

If improv is to rival scripted theater, we have to make it *more dangerous*, not safer. Seeking pleasure is dangerous. Following your impulses is always riskier than following a logical decision-making process.

And guess what else? When you improvise from your impulses, following your heart and body, you generate narrative that is more immediate and more gripping than anything your brain could create. To incite our audiences on a gut level, we've got to improvise from our guts. We lead the dance with the audience, we define the terms of engagement: intellect speaks to intellect, body to body, and heart to heart.

Following your body can affect narrative offers. Here's an example I saw in a class. In a Shakespeare scene, two sisters were arguing over a man, and who would wed him. A third sister urged family unity and other high moral ideals. When it was eventually revealed that the suitor had no money, the two sisters spurned him, although he was a good and kind man with a loving heart. After the first two sisters exited the stage, he was alone with the quiet and gentle third sister. The two improvisers looked at each other for a moment, and their bodies started moving closer together, but for some reason, both improvisers blocked these offers from their bodies, moved away from each other, and made overly complicated offers that took us away from the story. The audience was disappointed. All we needed was for them to follow the impulses they could feel

---

If improv is to rival scripted theater, we have to make it MORE DANGEROUS.

We lead the dance with the audience, we define the terms of engagement: intellect speaks to intellect, body to body, and heart to heart.

(and be joined together), and the scene would have had a satisfying and simple resolution. Instead, their brains took over and the end of the scene unraveled.

You'll be able to see this when it happens in others, and that will help prevent it from happening to you. As you work to let your body lead, pay attention to even the smallest movements, twitches, and gestures. If you begin a movement and pull back from it, you have more than likely just edited yourself. Let's say you're in a scene and you're seated and your partner is making very strong, provocative offers. You feel your butt twitch and you shift your weight in the chair ever so slightly. Your body wants to stand up, but for some reason, you won't let it. Go ahead. Stand up. Something on a gut level wants to move. And following these gut-level impulses kicks improv scenes into high gear. You know how I said your brain is not as smart as you think it is? Well, your butt is a lot *smarter* than you think it is. Follow your body—it knows what it's doing.

When your butt twitches, stand up.

Kirk Livingston, a friend and colleague of mine, puts it beautifully: "The body is the only part of us that exists only in the present moment. It can't be mired in the past or dreading the future. It only occupies the here and now." Therefore, your body is likely the only part of you that is always connected to the moment at hand. Let it be your guide.

The aim is for your work to be completely integrated—all your offers (physical, verbal and emotional) in alignment. We rely so heavily on our intellect that we often overlook valuable input we're receiving from our bodies. Nowhere is this truer than in improv scenes. And here's another fact: the audience sees everything. They see your butt twitch when your body wants to stand up; when you stay seated it looks weird to them and is unsettling on a subconscious level. If you stand up when your body wants to stand up, it's all so smooth and integrated that there's no disconnect between what the audience senses and what you do.

In this chapter I present several exercises to help you follow your body. Even though some of the exercises are performed with other players, your focus should be on your impulses and responses. This is the time to be self-centered, to seek the pleasure of being fully in your body.

Setting the Stage

The way you warm up affects everything that follows, so you should warm up the way you want to play. A fast-paced, mostly verbal warm-up will produce a quick and wordy show. A focused, body-first warm-up will give you the opportunity to connect with yourself before you speak and *before* you interact with anyone else. After the body is loose, we will warm up the voice and our "response muscles."

If you use the following warm-up, you can record the instructions to make things easier. Or you can create your own warm-up. Just be sure it's quiet and focused and performed fully.

The way you warm up affects everything that follows, so warm up the way you want to play.

Physical Warm-Up

Keep your breath moving freely throughout the warm-up. Lie on the floor, and bring your legs and feet together. Flex your feet, feeling the stretch along your calf muscles. Raise your arms over your head on the floor and stretch your arms and legs as far away from your body as possible.

Sweep your arms down (like a snow angel) along your body, bending your right knee into your chest. Grasp your bent knee with both arms and stretch your low back. Hold your right knee with your left hand and draw it across your body to the left, gently stretching your low back. Come back to center. Hold the right knee with the right hand and draw it to the right, stretching your inner groin muscle. Come back to center. Release the leg and straighten it back along the floor. Repeat with the left leg.

Draw both knees up and hug them to your chest. Drop the knees open (forming a diamond shape with your legs) and gently press your thighs open with your hands. Feel the stretch in the hip flexors. Bring your knees together and slowly lower them to the left, keeping them about two inches above the floor. Bring them back to center. Slowly lower them to the right, keeping them slightly off the floor. Bring them back to center. Hug them again to your chest. Keeping your knees bent, rock your body up into a sitting position.

Sit cross-legged on the floor. Inhale, raise your torso up from your hips, and twist gently to the right. Grasp your right knee with your left hand to help turn your body. Look over your right shoulder. Come back to center. Repeat on the left side. Come back to center.

Still sitting cross-legged on the floor, arch your back by lifting your head and curving your neck backward as you stretch your sternum toward the ceiling. While you are arched, bend forward from the waist and relax your back as you let your torso drop toward the floor. Relax and breathe. Repeat.

Slowly stand up. Stretch your arms over your head, reaching one toward the ceiling and then the other. Lower your arms. Raise your right arm; keeping your right arm straight, cross it over your body, using your left arm to stretch your shoulder. Repeat on the left side.

Relax your neck, rest your chin close to your chest and roll your head in half circles to the right, then to the left. Raise your head back up to center. Now look over one shoulder, then the other. Next, drop your right ear toward your right shoulder, then do it on the left side.

Massage

Pair up with a partner and decide who'll go first as you take turns giving each other a neck and shoulder massage. Once you've given/gotten feedback about how much pressure to use, settle into silence (play some soothing music if possible.) This is an opportunity to connect with your partner non-verbally and to focus yourself on each other in a caring way. If you're giving the massage, pay attention to your partner's response to your actions. If you find a knot of muscles, spend some time trying to work them out. If your partner is shifting painfully in her chair, adjust your movements accordingly. If you're receiving the massage, relax into it and focus on your breath: keep it moving slowly and rhythmically. Let the massage relax your mind as well as your body.

After three or four minutes, switch roles. Avoid the urge to talk during this exercise. Silence plus touch connects us in a deep way.

Vocal Warm-Up

This exercise is done first in a group. Stand in a circle. Your group will warm up your voices together in this call-and-response exercise. At the beginning of the exercise, remember to vocalize softly, in a barely audible whisper. As you proceed, you can gradually increase the volume and extend the pitches you are creating.

One person makes a very soft sound. The group mimics it. Another player makes a new sound. The group mimics it. Remember, these early sounds should be whispery soft. The call and response continues. Players add sounds in a random order. As the sounds become more robust, add a movement with each sound. Continue until the group is fully warmed up, or you collapse in a fit of giggles, whichever comes first.

In later workouts or classes, you will do this exercise with a partner, taking turns creating the new sounds.

Vocal Interaction

After you're thoroughly warmed up, pair up with someone and create a vocal interaction that doesn't involve words. Let your sounds and faces convey meaning. Even though you're not speaking words, the rhythm, musicality, and quality of your voice will add dimension to the interaction. You're not mirroring your partner now; you are interacting with him on a primitive vocal level. If this evolves to include physical offers, so much the better.

This next exercise allows us to practice action and reaction without having to worry about dialogue. Exaggerating our responses helps us define them fully; it's hard to wuss out on an offer if you're really stretching your arms, legs, torso and face.

It's also a great reminder of how fun it is to do something fully, without thinking.

Clown Responses

Players pair up for this silent exercise. Acting as clowns, one player (Player A) will make an offer, and Player B will respond. Each player should exaggerate every single offer. For instance, if my partner has just smiled at me, and my response is shyness, I will do a *clown* version of shyness, extending every part of myself as fully as possible: twisting my body away from him, clasping my hands firmly, dipping my head—anything a clown might do. My shyness is my offer back to my partner, who will respond fully.

Keep the interaction silent. Place your attention on your partner, and your responses to your partner's actions. Then follow through as thoroughly as possible. See if in the next moment you can go even further with your responses, or react more quickly. These interactions can be completely fanciful; don't worry about creating a linear narrative—you're simply acting and reacting.

PHYSICAL CHARACTERIZATIONS

Let's face it: we like to work in character because we can do strange things and nobody can blame *us*. That's an excellent reason to use strong character work as the basis for primitive responsiveness: if you cough on me and I slap you, hey, it's just my character doing it. Because *I* am far too genteel to slap anyone. And if someone else creates my character, I'm even less responsible for it. To free yourself from your usual constraints, try the following exercise. You'll be creating and exchanging characters with your partner. This exercise is especially useful in an ensemble where people are familiar with each other's work. Use this exercise to stretch your fellow players' character ranges; create characters and physicalities you would like to see them try.

Character Swap

Working in pairs, decide who will go first. Player A will create a character. Work from the ground up: start by moving around, experimenting with weight shifts, strides, bounces, etc. Let the character emerge from your feet, moving up the body. After you've captured the walk, move your torso, arms, and shoulders, until you find the movement for that particular character. Lastly add the neck, head and face. When you have completed the character, teach it to your partner. This will be her character for future exercises. As you teach your partner, pay close attention and side-coach if necessary: "She swings her arms more," or "Bounce your knees when you walk." Use phrases or images to convey the essence of the character to your partner. For instance, you might say, "Her body is always a question mark," or "He has a smile like peanut brittle."

Once your partner has mastered her new character, she will create a different character and teach it to you. Once you have both received your new characters, walk around the room and practice moving. See if any emotional or mental impulses come with the new persona. Lastly, find the voice. (*Note: the first few times players do this exercise, they tend to create freakish characters. As you play with the exercise, experiment with creating people you might see in everyday life. Then heighten them just a bit.*)

Character Interactions

Now you will create interactions between these new characters. This exercise is useful to watch, so do it in a performance setup: two players at a time, the rest of the group as audience.

Two players (who were not partners in the previous exercise) start an interaction using their new characters. This is a simple give-and-take exercise. If the interaction evolves into a scene, that's fine. The focus of the exercise is to act and react in character, paying particular heed to the body and what it wants. The two improvisers who created these characters act as coaches from the audience, calling out adjustments to keep the characters crisp and well defined. After a round of interactions, talk about what engaged you as an audience member: when did you sit forward? What made you respond? What seemed truthful? What struck a false note?

Moment from Life

This is a silent, solo exercise. Choose a meaningful moment from your life and re-create it for your fellow players. Before you begin, try to mentally capture the essence of the moment, especially its physical and emotional aspects. As you re-enact the moment, allow the time to let your actions have an effect on your inner life.

Any moment you remember vividly will work. In the past, I've seen the following, and all were very effective: a small boy is goaded into riding his bicycle down a steep hill; a mother loses her young child in a supermarket; a young adult boards a bus alone to move to California from the Midwest; a five-year-old pees her pants during a violin recital; a woman visits her friend (and brand-new baby) in the hospital.

It's best to choose a moment that didn't involve language, as you will be performing silently. After all the players have performed, discuss together what attracted your interest: at what points did you sit forward on your seat and feel yourself drawn into the story?

Following your body isn't limited to standing, sitting, and walking. Hands, arms, heads, shoulders, groins, feet—all our elements are constantly sending signals to the audience and us. Once you learn to follow your body, you'll find you're more relaxed on stage because you won't be fighting your instincts, which is incredibly hard work. If you're playing a character very different from yourself, the character may inhabit your body and send signals that are very new to you. This can be disconcerting at first, but find the courage to stay with it—you have lost yourself in the character and are probably playing in very new territory. Lucky you!

Once you learn to follow your body, you'll find you're more relaxed on stage because you won't be fighting your instincts, which is incredibly hard work.

One caveat here: in certain instances our bodies are in a fight-or-flight mode and we want to run away. In some scenes, for theatrical reasons, it would be better to stay planted firmly in the interaction and not move. In a case like this, the tension between what the body wants and what you are allowing it to do may increase the comedic or dramatic interest of the scene. As you experiment with following your physical instincts, you will come to recognize when to move and when to be still.

When you follow your body you are better able to express the emotional life of the character with your physical offers. When I'm directing improv (or scripted work), I may stop an actor and say, "You don't seem to be feeling anything." To which the actor often replies, "But I am, I'm feeling really sad." Unfortunately, if the audience can't see it, the emotion doesn't exist as far as they're concerned. It has to come *out* of you in your face, your body, and voice. It's our job as actors to express the internal world in an outward and visible way, so the audience can respond to it.

If you're self-conscious on stage and move more awkwardly than you would like, following your body will be a boon to you. If you tend to stand in one spot and talk until something funny comes out, you should also benefit from this work. If, on the other hand, you are already a centaur thundering through the woods, you shouldn't think about this too much or you may screw up a good thing.

Our bodies carry all the joy and heartache and humor and pathos we've ever experienced. The body knows what it means to be human. If we free ourselves physically we can lead the audience on a merry chase through the woods; we can take them back to their centaur roots and make them go all JELL-O in their chairs. Remember: we lead the dance. When we improvise from our bodies, hearts, and minds, we free the audience as well as ourselves.

When we improvise from our bodies, hearts, and minds, we free the audience as well as ourselves.

Getting Got
Revealing Emotion

There are no two ways about it: to create meaningful moments on stage, we've got to show emotion. And most of us expend a ton of energy avoiding that reality. Only in an improv scene can a woman be called ugly and just sit there as though nothing at all had been said.

Remember in chapter 3 I talked about how the body often responds instinctually and then the improviser quashes that response? I'm sure in the example above, the woman probably flinched ever so slightly, since most of us are not used to being called ugly on a regular basis. But if she flinched, she mashed it down and refused to acknowledge what her body already knew: that she had received a blow.

Which brings me to the concept of "getting got." Getting got means letting the audience see the arrow land. Remember playing cowboys and Indians as a kid? One kid yells, "Bang, Bang! I got you!" The other kid yells, "Did not! Did not!" Too many improv scenes suffer from the Did Not syndrome. You Did Not Hurt Me. You Did Not Best Me. You Did Not Make Me Smile.

The smart kids knew that it was more fun to clutch your ribs and do a few spins on your way to a really spectacular death than it was to stand and shout, "Did not!/Did so!" back and forth for an hour.

If only it was limited to not falling down when we got shot, I could let it go. But as an audience member, I'm actually more disappointed when *emotional* arrows aren't acknowledged. When Player A tells Player B that he doesn't love her anymore, and she just sits there, or worse yet, tosses it off and says, "I never loved you, either," I'm disappointed. It's not that this isn't realistic. It's that the improviser is staying safe, refusing to go into emotional territory that she would prefer to avoid.

As adults, we know the potential consequences of revealing our emotions. We know it's a risk to love, to trust, to fear or to betray another person. That's why it's doubly riveting to see an improviser, with all his awareness of the world's vagaries, follow his imagination and his heart.

What prevents us from doing this? Our *brains*. They want to wait and see, to choose a prudent, low-risk course of action. This is an impediment to vigorous improvising, because while you're busy judging, comparing, and choosing an emotion, you aren't listening to or connecting with your fellow players. But most importantly, it's a problem because it interferes with the natural rhythms of stimulus/response, and that's the reason life on stage so rarely resembles life in *life*.

OK, I admit—it's true that as adults in the "real world" we often mask our emotions (and for good reason, such as keeping our jobs or not getting smacked). However, those emotions come to us unbidden, and *unchosen*. If someone calls me an egomaniacal jerk, I don't decide how that makes me feel. I only decide after the fact if I'm going to reveal that emotion.

Remember: *we don't go to the theater to see life as it is. We go to the theater to see life as we wish it could be.* I believe that we wish people would be more honest in real life. I believe we wish we could be more open about our emotions. I believe we long to see the effect we have on others, and to show their effect on us.

There's nothing more surprising than someone admitting she's afraid. It's very satisfying to see a character lose face and show it. Or lose, period.

And what about winning? Where are all the scenes about joy, love, success, lust, wishes, dreams, and miracles? These positive human experiences are usually played out with even *less* enthusiasm and commitment than scenes about loss, grief, and

When you get shot with an emotional arrow, let the audience see it land.

We don't go to the theater to see life as it is. We go to see life as we wish it could be.

pain. I am constantly amazed at how seldom improvisers let their characters savor success. For example, an entire scene has centered on a woman overcoming discrimination to be hired for a job. As the scene is ending, she gets the job. Instead of celebrating, nine times out of ten, the improviser will lecture the boss on how he should have done it sooner. Instead of just *taking the win*. I'm often sidecoaching, "Take the win! Take the win! Celebrate your success!" It's weird how hard it is for people to be happy on stage.

On the other hand, is this so puzzling? How many people do you know who can tell you about something wonderful that has happened to them without mitigating it? I've started paying close attention to conversations (my own and my friends') and I've noticed a trend. Let's say a friend has had some time off from work and has been creating art, writing, and playing music. After talking about that very briefly, this friend may say, "But I've got to start thinking about making some money soon. I can't do this forever. I'll really be broke if I keep this up." Or these kinds of remarks, which come out of my mouth more than I'd like to admit: "We had the best time this weekend. We were so relaxed and happy, just doing whatever we wanted to do, when we wanted to do it. Today, though, I feel so behind in my work."

Would it kill me to stay a moment longer in my happiness? Is it absolutely necessary to jump immediately to what's wrong, or more oddly, what might go wrong? I think I know why we do this. One reason might be that we don't want to feel others' jealousy of our happiness, so we dilute it before they have a chance to be jealous. Another reason is a sort of knocking-wood to the gods: if I punish myself for my happiness, the gods won't.

Either way, it's a real energy-sucking experience. This kind of emotional diluting also sucks the life right out of scene work.

So what's the remedy? Well, there's no modifier like experience. It's the same as following your body: once you feel how powerful it is to free your emotions in public, you'll want to do it again. It's lovely to be overtaken by our own desires and dreams. A more liberating sensation can hardly be imagined. To practice in real life, try this: the next time you have something wonderful going on, imagine it's happening to someone else,

> *Let your character savor success.* **TAKE THE WIN.**

> *Once you feel how powerful it is to free your emotions in public, you'll want to do it again. It's lovely to be overtaken by our own desires and dreams.*

and celebrate on their behalf. Tell people about it; hope for more.

Seek love and success in scenes; be rapturous when you win and gracious when you lose. (If you're saying sarcastically to yourself, "Yeah, right, it's just *that* easy to overcome all my social training"—then try this on for size: you *have* to find a way to do it. You owe it to the audience. And the best way is to just do it.) Take action. Stop making excuses. Here's an exercise to get you started.

Seek love and success; be rapturous when you win and gracious when you lose.

Hot Objects

This exercise is best done after a few weeks of working together or if you are in an established ensemble. It's important to agree that the stories shared in this exercise are confidential and will not be discussed outside the group. Have people bring to rehearsal objects that have strong emotional significance for them. (Bring the actual objects.) Place a chair in front of the group and have one improviser get up and sit in the chair with her object. Ask her to describe it objectively, as though she was a stranger looking at it. For example, if it's a pocket watch, she may say, "This is a large, round pocket watch made of silver. It is engraved with a vine pattern on the cover. Inside, the face is made of mother-of-pearl." And so on. After she has described the object in this way, ask her to tell the group why it is important to her. Each person's turn should last no more than five minutes. (I never time anyone, but just giving the parameters of five minutes seems to keep the exercise manageable.) Before beginning the exercise, ask the class to refrain from applauding at the end of each story. Since these are stories from real life (and we can't know the content before we begin), it's awkward to applaud. After each player has finished, the group or leader can simply thank the player.

I have done this exercise with lots of groups, and it always proves useful. It's impossible to predict the outcome of the exercise, but it consistently provides three benefits: 1) We get the opportunity to experience and express emotions in public. 2) We understand from an audience perspective how it feels to listen to truthful, emotional work. 3) We are able to observe how emotion shapes language and physicality. When they're affected by their hot objects, the players may pause, start, stop, and start again, shift, cry, laugh—all without choosing or deciding to do so.

After everyone has done the exercise, the group can discuss what they observed. Leave the content of the stories out of the discussion; otherwise your conversation may be overtaken by comments such as, "I really liked it when you talked about how your grandfather sold the farm." The content of the stories is not important for our purposes. Instead, the group should talk about when they were moved as an audience, what caused them to sit forward with interest—what was going on in that moment. For example, someone may say, "I found I was always interested when the person looked at their object—they really seemed to be connected to the memory in those moments."

Personally, I'm always interested in what the player chooses *not* to say; those moments of privacy are often very full. For reasons of his own the player chooses not to share something with us, and that choice almost always involves a struggle. As audience members, it is the *struggle* that intrigues us—not the resolution.

The hot object exercise teaches us that words are the least important manner of conveying emotional information. Very often, it's not the words themselves that move us; rather, it's the *effect* the object has on the player. Some of the most memorable hot objects I've seen involved very little speaking.

This exercise also builds ensemble. In addition to the performance benefits, we have the opportunity to peer into each other's lives. After experiencing and observing emotionally driven behavior, we can begin to incorporate emotional responsiveness into our scene work. To make space for this to emerge, we need to slow down a bit. With practice, emotions can be accessed in real time and you won't have to sacrifice the pace of a scene to fill it with feeling.

Emotion has a better chance of emerging and expressing itself in silence. This next exercise lets you practice interacting silently with a partner.

Silent Scenes

Two players improvise a short, silent scene. Try to play realistically and avoid worrying about the narrative. This is a simple exercise to respond emotionally and physically to your partner. If a story emerges let it grow out of the interaction between you. Your focus should be on feeling your responses and letting them show through your facial expressions and body language. If your partner in the scene seems menacing, move away from him. If you are in love with him, move closer. The idea isn't to feign an interaction, but to actually intersect with your partner.

After playing one round this way, add language to the scenes. Continue to let your face and body do most of the talking, with only occasional help from your lips. Avoid the urge to explain how you're feeling; let us see it instead.

I learned this next exercise from SAK Theater in Orlando. In addition to being a great rehearsal exercise, it works well in performance. I'm very fond of it for character work, and it's also an effective way to explore the emotional aspects of improvising.

Orlando Monologues

Three improvisers will participate in this cycle of monologues. They get a suggested object from the audience; all three players will use the same suggestion

The first improviser walks onstage, mimes picking up the object, and tells a short improvised story (in character) about why the object is important to him. The player should strive to make an emotional connection with the object before speaking, or be affected by it during the course of his monologue. He then stands up, places the object back on the chair, and exits the stage.

The second player enters, picks up the object, and begins to tell another story about the object, somehow connected to the first. For example, perhaps in the first monologue we learned that the silver spoon was owned by the very old lady we saw talking. In the second scene, we may be hearing from her granddaughter, to whom the spoon passed upon the grandmother's death. Again, the second improviser should focus on having an emotional inner life that the object inspires.

The third improviser enters and proceeds as did the other two. This last monologue should reveal yet a third element of the story. It's ideal if the three stories are intertwined, but for our purposes here, don't worry too much about the narrative factor. Instead, use the exercise to be emotionally affected by not only the object, but also the other stories.

Place your focus on inward stillness and then remain open to the thoughts and emotions that arise within you. The following example arose in a class several years ago. The suggestion was a music box.

Player A (a man) talked about getting the box as a gift when he was a child, and how much it meant to him. The story was told very simply; the improviser didn't push for emotion, but trusted in truthful behavior to convey his feelings.

Player B was his wife, talking about their little girl, who always danced to the music box when the husband played it. The little girl had been killed in a car accident years ago.

Player C (a woman, playing a young girl) came out, wound the music box up, and listened to it for a moment. Then she smiled at the audience and told us all the things she wanted to do when she grew up. The actor was beautiful and full of light, and gave herself over completely to embodying the little girl. It was a deeply moving piece and it worked because the actors weren't afraid to be emotional.

This is a terrific format with a lot of flexibility. I have seen the following variations:

- Each improviser plays the same character at a different stage in life
- The action moves backward in time
- Each improviser plays a different emotional *aspect* of one character (for instance: fear, lust, and joy)

Feel free to experiment with the form. Remember, as with the Hot Objects, it's often what a character *shows* us that reveals who she is. The most poignant or funny moments in Orlando Monologues often occur *between* the lines.

Dealing with Difficult Emotions

Most of us don't consciously seek out pain, yet in a scene we may be required to feel pain as our character gets put through his or her paces. Scenes may produce strong emotions that we don't care to experience. Well, guess what? You can't be fully effective unless you are willing to experience the whole range of human emotion. The audience paid its money to watch someone else be embarrassed, happy, lusty, or vengeful. And you don't get to hold back just because it's uncomfortable.

Here's a secret: it's not happening to you. It's happening to the character to whom you've lent your body. Unless you're psychologically unbalanced (in which case I don't recommend improvising), you'll not only weather your character's emotional upheavals, but you may find it freeing, even fun. You may be surprised at the deep pleasure of improvising with your whole, truthful self—even in a scene that's emotionally painful. If you feel that you're holding the audience's hearts in your hands, you will be able to commit to the emotional reality in order to serve them. If you can tell that your partner is deeply moved by your mutual creation, you will be filled with the greatest joy an improviser can know. That you may also experience a personal catharsis is a side benefit.

The audience wants us to be braver than they are. If improvisation is to fulfill its promise as a performance medium, we have to be brave in a new way. Our risk-taking has to go beyond doing a scene in reverse, or showing off our skills at speaking in rhyme. Emotional terrain is still largely unexplored in improvisation, and that expedition is long overdue.

You must be willing to experience the whole range of human emotion. The audience paid its money to watch someone else be embarrassed, happy, lusty, or vengeful. You don't get to hold back just because it's uncomfortable.

The audience wants us to be braver than they are.

Pushing Your Partner
Improv Etiquette

Up to this point, you've been probing your inner workings; now you're going to turn your attention outward. In the next section of the book you'll be looking at how to connect with and be affected by your improv partners. This is exciting and dangerous work. We've laid the foundation for trust, and now that trust will be tested. Since you'll be nudging each other into unfamiliar territory, it behooves me to point out some practical and social niceties. Some of these suggestions revolve around physical safety and mutual respect; others will set you free to play fully and with fire.

PHYSICAL BOUNDARIES

Make sure you and your partners are aware of any physical limitations anyone has and map out the parameters before you begin working together. If someone has a bad knee, go gently. It's easy to get carried away; safety should always be your paramount concern. Be careful when stage fighting. No hitting or tossing your partner. You get the drift.

Also pay attention to your partners' comfort level in other kinds of physical exercises and scenes. If the scene calls for a kiss, do it demurely. Avoid the urge to go on a search-and-destroy mission with your tongue.

Ditto physical contact of a sexual nature. If you're playing a seduction scene, stay within the boundaries of normal touching. If you are part of an ensemble, working with people who have developed a high level of trust, these boundaries may be expanded. But start slowly, and take your cue from your partner. Men in particular need to be aware that their view of appropriate contact and a woman's view may be quite different.

NOTES

Don't give unsolicited input to other improvisers. Just don't. If a fellow player asks for feedback, expound away. But don't assume anyone wants your two cents unless they ask for it. Now, having said that, you should receive notes as part of your regular practice sessions. Here's my take on notes: they work best when a director gives them. If you work in a collective, take turns directing (and whoever is directing the run should not perform in those shows). The director sits objectively outside the process and sees what the audience sees; his comments are the most useful if your goal is to give your audience the best show you can. Set up a system where notes are integrated into your rehearsal process.

Take any notes you get with grace and good humor. Avoid the urge to argue with notes, as this is an enormous waste of time. Take the note, think about it a bit, and incorporate it the next time you work. Try it more than once, more than one way. If, upon reflection and practice, you decide the note isn't valid, kiss it goodbye.

Lastly, avoid giving notes after shows. During a performance, the energy of the players is moving outwardly, to each other and to the audience. After the show, this outward flow of energy continues. Listening to notes is a drawing-in process and runs counter to the momentum in the room. Also, scene-by-scene notes tend to address moments that are gone forever. It's useless to tell someone, "You missed the offer of the raincoat." That moment is *gone*. Over. Finito.

Your director should take notes at your shows. Have him look for players' patterns and tendencies rather than making detailed notes of every scene. He can then make constructive

If the scene calls for a kiss, do it demurely. Avoid the urge to go on a search-and-destroy mission with your tongue.

suggestions for change at the next rehearsal, which is a more appropriate setting.

When you're finished with a show, congratulate each other and go get a soda.

Two Kinds of Polite

Most beginning improv training involves the concept of making your partner look good. That's cool. The trouble is, the idea often gets transmuted along the way into what I call being a co-dependent improviser, and that leads to all sorts of problems. Let's look at two kinds of polite behavior: the right kind and the kind that just messes everything up.

Making your partner look good doesn't mean being co-dependent.

The Right Kind of Polite

The right kind of polite consists of being generous, leaving room for your partner, listening and responding as fully as possible, playing characters truthfully and with abandon. You make your partners look good by giving them good, strong offers to play with, by reinforcing their offers and building on them, and by having as much fun as you possibly can.

Being the right kind of polite means that you will *make use* of every offer. It does not mean you will dance a jig of joy over every offer or that your character will like everything that happens to her in a scene. It involves responding fully and truthfully to each offer your partner makes. You'll never ignore an offer if you are the right kind of polite.

Let's say you're in a scene as a lost tourist on a tropical island. A band of natives has taken you to the top of the volcano and you are told you will be thrown in as a sacrifice to the gods. You are not required to say, "Great, toss me in!" Your job is to respond fully to the offer, which can include kicking, screaming and trying to escape. These enrich the scene.

What confuses a lot of improvisers is the concept of blocking. You don't want to block your partner. Good for you; blocking is bad. But remember that a block is a denial of the reality of an offer, such as "I'm immortal" or "that's not a volcano." It's not blocking to be unhappy about something. Go ahead—have strong feelings about things. You must simply make use of every offer.

Similarly, when you are making offers that affect your partner's character, don't limit yourself to making that character comfortable. If I'm in a scene playing a young child who's come home with a bad report card, and my mother says, "Your father's had a bad day at work," that is a HUGE gift to me. I now have a lot of emotional territory to play in before my father even comes on stage. I may try to hide my report card, tear it up, or alter it; I may decide to run away from home, or paint a picture for my father to mollify him. And when he does arrive in the scene, our interaction will already have some substance to it, because the actor playing my mother had the courage to make my character uncomfortable.

If, on the other hand, she had said, "Well, that's OK, sweetie, your father is pretty understanding about these things," what's the point of my having made the offer about the bad report card? If it's going to be FINE with everybody that I'm a crummy student, the offer gets nullified. And that's what I mean by co-dependent improvising. Just like in life, the poor behavior gets reinforced as everyone around the person with the problem scurries to take away the consequences of that behavior.

In the example of the report card scene, if Tom is playing the father, he now has carte blanche to be the father from hell—because that will best serve the scene. It will also be the biggest gift to me, as it will increase my dilemma, and make the comedy (or drama) richer. If I'm trying to hide my report card in the closet, and my father is set on looking in the closet for his golf clubs, then Tom is doing me a big favor. If he sits quietly on the couch, why did we bother with the previous offers?

The Wrong Kind of Polite

The wrong kind of polite consists of sitting on your instincts because you don't want to be a stage hog, playing nice characters all the time, saying yes when you feel like saying no, or wussing out on characterizations and offers.

These choices are untruthful. Stage hog worry involves turning a deaf ear to your creative imagination. Playing nice characters all the time is false on its face. Always saying yes denies your internal reality in favor of a rule. Wussiness is about not playing to your full potential because you're afraid. Fear is rarely a truthful motivator. Let's knock these puppies down one at a time.

Stage Hog

While it's true that nobody likes a stage hog, everybody likes an improviser who plays strongly and well, and who comes in when needed. The key to avoiding stage-hogdom is to make sure that other people are contributing to the scene as much as you are. If you're doing all the talking, or using all your skills to highlight your character, then you may, in fact, be a big fat pig. If, on the other hand, you are acting on your impulses and making offers that highlight other characters, if you are helping push the story forward, or clarifying the action, you are not a stage hog, but are in fact a wonderful person and a delightful improviser.

Playing Nice Characters All the Time

If you're caught up worrying about what other people will think of you, then you're no longer serving the scene; instead, you're focusing on your own self-image. Improv as therapy is an accidental phenomenon. The fact that we get to learn about ourselves is a beneficial by-product of the process, but while on stage, our responsibility is to the audience. Soooo, if you were raised to always make nice, that's an interesting but irrelevant issue when you're performing. If the scene needs a villain, play the baddest, meanest, most morally bankrupt villain you can. *It's great fun.* And talk about therapeutic!

In addition to out-and-out villains, scenes often need characters who pose obstacles to the protagonist. It's hard to do a good job posing obstacles if you are trying to be *nice* all the time.

Saying Yes When You Should Say No

There's an art to knowing when you should say No in a scene. This goes beyond being unhappy about things—this is literally about the word "No." You should say no when your instincts tell you to. I'll give you some examples. At the very top of a scene, two men were onstage. Dave was seated, looking uncomfortable. Pete was standing and fiddling with a space-object tool of some kind.

> *If you're caught up worrying about what other people will think of you, then you're no longer serving the scene. Making nice is for the Ladies' Auxiliary.*

Dave: Is this going to hurt?"

Pete: Yes! ["*Yippee!*" *thought the audience*]

Dave: But you've done this procedure before, right? [*More worried now*]

Pete: Yes, lots of times.

The audience sat back in our chairs, disappointed. In this instance, "No" would have been a much stronger choice, not only because it would heighten Dave's dilemma, but because it would have been a fuller acceptance of his implied offer. When Pete said, "Yes, I've done it lots of times," all the meaning and interest drained out of the scene like oil out of an old Chevy.

Say "No" when it pushes the story forward.

When I was a very green improviser, I was in a scene with one of my idols, and he was the bad guy (I was the protagonist, although I don't think I knew it at the time). He pulled a gun on me in the library of my father's house. I had a diamond necklace in my hands, and he wanted it. With a gun pointed at me, he yelled menacingly, "Give me the diamonds or I'll shoot you!" I somehow had the presence of mind to say "No." He then shot me and all hell broke loose, and the scene was really great. After the show he said, "I was so glad you knew to say no to me in that scene—if you had said yes, it would have ruined everything!"

We sometimes say no for the wrong reasons—often we're stalling because we're afraid of what might happen in the next moment. With practice you will learn when "No" will serve the story, and will begin to trust your instincts more.

Wussing

The wrong kind of polite leads to tippy-toeing, which ruins scenes. A wuss makes poorly defined offers and plays half-baked characters. This happens for a couple of reasons: 1) We don't have the courage to make a full, complete and strong offer because we're worried it's wrong, or 2) We're afraid our partner won't like our offer. Whatever the reasons for limp offers, they hurt scenes. And guess what? They hurt scenes more than really dumb or bizarre offers. Even dumb offers, if they're made with gusto, can be utilized.

Let's say in a scene a man goes to the doctor and says, "I don't feel well." The doctor asks, "What seems to be the problem?" and the patient replies, "Well, it's nothing too bad. Actually, I'm not even sure I needed to come see you at all." What in heaven's name is the doctor supposed to do with that? Now he has to come up with some ailment, and all because the improviser was too wussy to follow through on his *own* offer—that there is something wrong with him. It would be much more helpful if the patient said, "I can't stop itching," or "My eyeball keeps falling out," or *anything*, so long as it's a clean, clear and strong offer.

I think we mistakenly believe that it's impolite to be definitive, that it's somehow more polite to make our partners do all the work. Maybe we believe that then they will be happy, because they will be creating the scene the way they want it to go. But nobody likes doing all the work in scenes. Trust me. Your partners will be happier if you pull your share of the load.

Another weakling approach is to play poorly defined characters. These tend to take on the characteristics of those around them, and pretty soon you've morphed into your partner's character. I call this merging—when two people meld into one. It happens a lot at the beginning of scenes. Let's say two characters are sitting on a park bench. One person is eating a sandwich; the other is trying to read. Nine times out of ten, instead of staying with these activities, both characters will drop them and start talking. Within seconds of starting a conversation, they will lose their distinguishing characteristics, and become essentially the same character. The next common occurrence is that the scene will not seem to be "about" anything, and both actors will start thrashing wildly. This usually leads to a whole bunch of offers, and the scene is probably doomed.

If, however, the person reading is fastidious, very prim and proper, and the person eating the sandwich is a slob and quite outgoing, now we have the makings for an interesting interaction, without having to search for unrelated offers.

Sometimes the reverse happens, and the players mirror each other from the outset of the scene. It's important that characters be differentiated from one another throughout scenes if we are to have any hope of creating a story from the interaction. For example, two players have gotten the suggestion "brothers" from the audience. The scene starts, and we learn that the mother of these men has just died. If the players mirror each other, sharing the same emotional states, needs, etc.,

To create a story from an interaction, characters must be differentiated from one another throughout the scene.

they will find it hard going to create a story. If, however, they are quite different from one another (if one is quiet and composed, and the other loud and emotional), they will likely discover that the scene unfolds effortlessly.

Here's an interesting fact: when we are fully in our bodies, we *never mirror* because we are playing from our own inner truth. If I'm a happy character in a scene, and my partner is also happy, we will still be different because we each manifest happiness in our own way. I believe we tend to mirror because it feels safe. Stop playing it safe and focus instead on creating crisp, delineated characters that rub up against each other.

Playing from Within

If you play fully in your body you'll NEVER MIRROR *because you will be playing from your unique inner truth.*

There's so much to lose track of when improvising. Names, objects, narrative offers—these can be as ephemeral as a fruit fly. You can't know what's in your partner's mind when she makes an offer; you can't know what she's hoping for, and it's a waste of time to try. But you *can* know what's going on inside your character, your body, and your mind. If you simply respond to offers from that knowledge, you will be adding to the truthfulness of the scene and, very likely, to the strength of the story.

Your most generous act is a strong offer. Your best contribution is a clearly defined character who remains distinct. If you can do these things, people will be eager to play with you, because you will be easy and fun to play with.

Active Investment vs. Passive Tolerance

One of my class goals from the very beginning was to create an atmosphere in which artistic excellence and individual growth were sustained by a vital group energy. This goes beyond merely creating a safe environment—it requires generosity of spirit and conscious effort from everyone in the group.

One of the ways we pursue this end is to make each individual's goal public. When everyone in the class knows the purpose and challenges for his or her fellows' work, each player can be an active participant in that work. Students are expected not merely to sit politely and watch scenes, but to push their partners into new territory, to offer help getting there, and to applaud them when they arrive.

Making our goals public is not an easy thing to do. It means admitting, in so many words, "I'm not good at this," or at least, "I'm not as good at this as I want to be." It also raises the stakes as we begin to work, because we have chosen to work at something we feel ill equipped to pursue. And we're doing it in front of other people. In class we make our goals public to take the stigma out of learning new skills.

In my classes, at the beginning of each eight-week session, each of us (including me) states our goal to the rest of the group. I've noticed that just saying mine out loud makes me relax a little. Once the goals have been stated and recorded, we get on with our work.

This model has worked very well. As each individual becomes more skilled, the overall quality of the scene work improves, which makes class more fun to be part of. As class is more fun, people feel freer to take chances, the scene work improves, and the cycle becomes self-perpetuating.

Working this way has another benefit. Instead of each of us focusing inwardly on our own goal, we have placed our focus outside ourselves, on the work as a whole. This enables us to be more objective not only about the work of others, but about our own efforts, and the active support we feel helps us take greater risks.

We need to trust other people in order to take risks. We can't control the trustworthiness of others, of course. But we can learn how to be trustworthy *ourselves*, which adds to the whole. The quality of being worthy of trust is a real gift in an improviser. How do we embody this? By being generous, non-judgmental and willing to participate in an experiment. It means remembering our own shortcomings, our own challenges, and using empathy to support and uplift our fellow players. Above all, it means taking risks. It entails being willing to fail and look ridiculous. When we risk ourselves publicly, we add immeasurably to the trust level of the group.

A note here: being trustworthy doesn't mean doing your partners' work for them. It doesn't mean that you will try to take their discomfort away during times of exploration. In fact, it often means that you will push them (gently) into the territory

Being trustworthy doesn't mean doing your partners' work for them.

they wish to enter, with the assurance that you will support them, whatever the outcome.

If you want to be polite all the time, join the Ladies' Auxiliary. Good, strong theater needs good, strong improvisers to provoke responses in each other. Embody the truth and insist on getting the truth in return. Don't settle for polite, wussy, lifeless scenes. When you work from your gut it's a whole new ball game.

Embody the truth and insist on getting the truth in return.

Long Time No Talk
Making Magic in Silence

It's easy to think we're not contributing if we're not talking, and unfortunately we improvisers seem to have some sort of pact that the stage will never be silent. And that's too bad because in silence all sorts of gooey, prickly, uncomfortable, comic, frightening, and dramatic moments lurk. The second we open our mouths those possibilities scurry away, and with them, the risk of the unknown.

So we talk to stay safe. And we talk to stay unaffected by the events of the scene. I honestly don't see how improv can fulfill its promise of adventure until we learn how to dive into silence and meet our partners there.

Here's what can happen if you will be quiet for a minute. You can:

- look into your partner's eyes and be affected by what you see
- feel your own emotional life within you and act on it
- pay attention to your body and follow it
- breathe

- get a grip if the scene is out of control and find a way to correct its course
- follow your instincts

If those aren't enough good reasons, here are some more:

- your partner can get a word in edgewise
- something unexpected can happen
- the audience can catch up with the story
- everyone's ears will get a rest

A sidecoaching remark I make a lot is "Leave room." This is my nice way of saying "Shut up." But it's actually more than a euphemism. I really do mean to leave room. Leave room in the scene for something emotional to happen to you, and for you to express it. Leave room for the *connection* between you and your partner, which is a separate entity if you give it enough space to emerge and grow. Leave room for the unexpected.

This isn't merely directed at people who drive the scene by talking too much. This is aimed at all of us. Most of us overtalk our offers. We say the same thing four times. We don't trust that we've made ourselves clear the first time, which we usually have. We make a good, strong remark and then embellish it with extra verbiage. See—I'm doing it now.

Once you're quiet, making meaningful eye connection is the next skill to practice. This involves more than looking into your partner's eyes. Like all our connective acts, it involves sending and receiving information. Not hard data, but subtler, less tangible information about ourselves. This requires openness to revealing oneself, as well as a willingness to see *into* someone else, to the degree they want to let us in.

Is this touchy-feely? Yup. Most improv I see has neither touch nor feeling, and it's time we found a way to incorporate human connection and tenderness into improvisation. The world is hungry for connection. We can provide it in scenes, for our audiences and ourselves. Silence is the foundation for connection, out of which grow compassion, longing, lust, hate, and fear—all the powerful human emotions that propel scenes.

Most of us get very little practice looking into other peoples' eyes. Try this experiment the next time you're out running

Leave room. Leave room for emotion, connection, and the unexpected.

Most improv has neither touch nor feeling. It's time we found a way to incorporate human connection and tenderness into improvisation.

errands: look into the eyes of the cashier at the store, the waiter who's serving you lunch, or the person standing next to you in line. Try to connect with them, to get them to look into your eyes if even for a moment, and see what happens to the quality of the interaction.

Luckily, in improv we can create the practice we need. The following series of exercises will let you connect with your partner and create interactions together that exist on the plane just below the spoken word.

Eye Connection Exercise 1

Choose a partner and sit facing each other, fairly close together. One player starts conveying a simple feeling, attitude or thought to his partner. The partner's job is only to look and receive the feeling. This exercise is done in silence. Once the partner thinks she knows what the feeling is, she nods, and it is her turn to send. Do this about three times each. This is a very simple, basic exercise. Don't attempt to convey complicated stories to one another. When each person has sent and received three separate feelings, or attitudes, compare notes with your partner and see how close you came to understanding one another.

Eye Connection Exercise 2

This is based on Viola Spolin's classic mirroring exercise. Two players stand facing each other, about two feet apart. Stand in a relaxed manner and look into each other's eyes for one or two minutes. This may feel odd. It's very rare that we look at anyone for two solid minutes, let alone near strangers. Stay with it. You may find some very interesting things begin to happen.

After a few minutes, one player begins to move very slowly, and the other player mirrors those movements. Player A (the leader) moves very slowly and fluidly; the goal is to make Player B look like a brilliant follower. After a few minutes, Player B will be the leader, and Player A will follow. Keep your visual connection during these changeovers.

As you and your partner work together, experiment by taking the movement into your entire bodies. If you have been working mostly with your hands and arms, try shifting your weight, bending your legs and exploring different levels. Maintain your eye connection at all times. Note any changes you feel internally as a result of the connection with your partner. Take several minutes to do the exercise.

In the third phase of the exercise, when you look at your partner, imagine you're looking at your own reflection in the mirror. Those eyes you see are your eyes. That hair is your hair. Those shoulders, your shoulders. Then imagine that you aren't quite sure which is the real you, and which is the reflection. Keep your eyes on you/your reflection as you begin to move, and notice any changes in the feeling of the exercise, or the qualities of the movements.

Eye Connection Exercise 3

It's useful for one person to act as the "caller" for this exercise. Start with these suggestions and make your own list of suggestions based on the needs of your group. The improvisers stand in two lines facing each other, so that each improviser is looking into a partner's eyes. Take a breath together, exhale together, and relax into looking at each other. The caller says, "Look for comfort in your partner's eyes." The improvisers connect with each other and relax into the goal. After a few moments, one line shifts down one person, so that everyone is looking at a new partner. Now the caller says, "Look for whimsy in your partner's eyes." The line shifts. "Look for mischief in your partner's eyes." The caller should allow enough time for the improvisers to settle into the connection with their partners, and to make discoveries while looking at one another. This is not a "sending" exercise. You simply look for what you need in your partner's eyes and see if you can find it there.

You may find yourself laughing during the exercise. That's fine. Keep your connection through your eyes and find your composure together with your partner.

Avoid pulling away to compose yourself. The point is to stay connected no matter what.

The Go Game

The Go Game can be used to illustrate more than one improv point; here we will be using it to look at connection and flow in a group.

Round One (standard play): Players stand in a circle. Someone (Player A) points to another player (B). By doing this, Player A is asking for permission to walk to Player B's position in the circle. Player B then says, "Go" (giving permission), and Player A walks to Player B. Player B now points to someone else, who says, "Go," and Player B walks to his or her spot in the circle, and so on.

Round Two: (pointing/nodding): Play continues in the same manner, except that now players will simply nod their heads instead of saying the word "Go."

Round Three (making faces): Play continues in the same manner, except that the players now forego pointing. To ask permission to move, a player will make eye contact with another player, make a face, and the responding player will make a face to indicate permission is granted. Have fun with it.

Round Four (eye connection): In this, the final iteration of the game, signaling between players consists only of eye connection. Now a player looks into the eyes of another player. With that, the transaction is complete, and the first person may begin moving to the other's position. Player B now looks into the eyes of another player, and moves to their position. This is the subtlest version of the game. Eye connection with your partner is critically important for the flow of the game. Avoid lifting the eyebrows, nodding, or any other physical indication that you are giving permission. Trust that if you are looking into the eyes of your partner, she understands what you mean and will act accordingly.

This round moves much more quickly than the verbal or even the face-making rounds, because non-verbal communication is so much faster than pointing and talking.

Also, by this round, the players understand the flow of the game, and more than one person may be moving at a time. It's amazing how fast eye contact can move through the circle.

In Round Four, mistakes may occur. As everyone is looking around the circle, people are bound to think they are being signaled, and begin to move. You may have several people moving at the same time, which usually means there's been a miscommunication. The players should stay relaxed, continue playing, and try to get the game back to its original flow. This might mean that one player will not move (if there are multiple transactions underway), or that someone needs to start a new transaction if the flow has stopped.

Let's back up a bit and talk about the game from the first round. When players are first learning this game, it looks so simple they are often surprised to find it difficult. These are the most common problems I've noted in the early stages of learning the game:

1. Players don't say "Go" when they are being pointed at. Remind yourselves that this is a permission game, and that your partner can't move until you say "Go."

2. Players say "Go" to give permission, and then point at someone else and say "Go" simultaneously. This one tends to be a brain-fry problem, and usually works itself out after a few practice rounds. I also think it has to do with the fact that we always want to talk to accomplish things. It's a good opportunity for us to practice physical offers.

3. A player who has just said "Go" moves towards someone else without asking for or receiving permission to move. This is probably the most common occurrence I see, and I think it stems from a sort of over-achiever syndrome. It's like the player is thinking, "I've just said 'Go.' It's my turn to move—here

I come!" But this player has forgotten that the purpose of the game is to work with other players to create movement together—not for each player to take off in a different direction, unconnected to the rest of the group.

4. One or two people can't play the game successfully no matter how hard they try. This usually seems to be a matter of nerves or tension. It sometimes helps to break the game back down into its parts. Have everyone practice the first step: pointing at someone. Then have everyone practice the second step: saying "Go" when you're pointed at, etc. I've found that eventually everyone is able to play this game, although it sometimes takes a few tries over a period of weeks. I never play the game past anyone's tolerance for failure.

After you've successfully played the game in its final form, talk about what you noticed during the game. How does the exercise simulate transactions in scenes? What kinds of things did you do in the game (helpful or not) that you do in scenes? How does the idea of completing transactions affect scene work?

Here's my answer to that last question. I believe a lot of scene problems can be solved if we understand the idea of completing the transaction at hand before moving on to the next one. Completing transactions helps us to use the offer in front of us, instead of adding a bunch of new ideas. Finding endings to stories also becomes much easier if we understand that stories are transactions that need to be completed. Look for questions that need answers, bargains to fulfill or break, relationships to begin or end.

Physical Connection

When it comes to physical connection, improv is at a real disadvantage compared to scripted theater. In scripted theater, the movements are designed, set, and rehearsed under the eye of the director. In improv we're all lucky not to be careening into the furniture most of the time. It's amazing that there aren't more injuries during improv performances.

In scripted scenes, touch (or the lack of it) is used to express a huge range of human emotional states: anger, love, lust, tenderness, uncertainty, bitterness, longing, joy, etc. The actors have time to integrate movement into the lives of their characters and the opportunity to practice more risky situations such as seduction or stage fighting. Improvisers have none of these luxuries. We can, however, practice using touch in workshop situations, which will make us more likely to use the full range of touch when we're in front of audiences.

Back to Back

Players pair up and stand back to back. This is a silent exercise. You should be leaning slightly against your partner, but supporting your own weight. Close your eyes. Keep them closed during the entire exercise. The first person who shifts his weight has begun the exercise. That is the first offer. When you feel your partner move, you should respond by moving. Remain in physical contact with your partner at all times. As you work together, you can experiment with shifting the weight between you. It's not necessary to stay back to back, but you must maintain a constant physical connection.

Pay attention to any sensations that arise during the exercise. You may have emotional responses to the work, or you may find that stories are suggested in the movements you create with your partner.

Perform the exercise for several minutes. Then slowly, working in concert with your partner, find your way back to your starting positions (back to back). Slowly separate from your partner, turn around, and open your eyes.

Contact/Non-Contact[4]

This exercise can be done with or without music. (If you're using music, soft instrumentals seem to work best.) Stand face to face with your partner, about two

---

4. This is an adaptation of an exercise created by Phil Porter and Cynthia Winton-Henry for their work, InterPlay.

feet apart. Begin moving (not mirroring each other) and come into physical contact with each other. For instance, you may touch your right wrist to your partner's left arm. When you find a moment of physical connection, hold it and relax into it. Hold it slightly longer than feels comfortable and see if the connection changes in any way. Then release, and move until you find the next moment of connection together.

You may want to begin with hand-to-hand contact, as this is the most comfortable when you're working with a new partner. As you become more relaxed with each other, explore connections with other parts of your body. Always pay attention to whether or not your partner seems comfortable. Look for the ways in which your *partner* wants to connect with *you*. This way, neither of you will be driving the transaction.

Now repeat the exercise without making actual physical contact. This time, you are still looking for moments of connection that you can click into and hold, but you won't be touching your partner physically. Experiment with how close together you can get without touching. How far apart can you move and still feel connected?

Do the exercise one more time. In this round, you will move in and out of physical contact, while you continue to find moments of connection with your partner.

This next exercise can be a very powerful experience if the trust level is high enough. Do be mindful that people have different levels of comfort with physical contact, and be respectful of those differences.

Hands On

Sit facing your partner. Close your eyes, and begin touching each other's hands. Go slowly. You may find that you and your partner limit your contact to hands, or you may find that as you work together you are able to explore other parts of the body. Move slowly and pay attention to your own needs, as well as those of your partner. If you are paying attention, you will be able to discern your comfort levels. This is a very intimate exercise and is likely to bring up a lot of strong feelings, many of which may be challenging for you. Let courage lead you. You shouldn't do anything that makes you too uncomfortable, but do let yourself venture a bit outside your ordinary comfort zone. Continue the exercise for five or so minutes.

Once you incorporate touch into scenes, you may wonder how you did without it all these years.

Once you incorporate touch into scenes, you may wonder how you did without it all these years. Experiment with how touch can work in a scene about longing, or unrequited love. One person craves the touch of another, who withholds it. It can be extremely moving and haunting to see the absence of touch.

A note about improv sex: most improv sex consists of what I call bunny-humping. Two players grab each other and start pounding pelvises at a rapid rate. Very odd and not very pretty to watch. Much more riveting (and riskier) are slow seduction scenes or scenes about first kisses, where the space between players ebbs and flows as the delicious tension builds. Be brave. Dare to be touched slowly.

Touch is one of the many ways to set theatrical improvisation apart from improv performed in bars or on television. If we can reach out to one another for comfort or support, in anger, lust, and joy, we can physically represent the audience's desires, dreams, and nightmares.

Through touch, we can physically represent the audience's desires and experience, and help play out their dreams and nightmares.

I'll never forget an experience I had when I was in high school. I was a volunteer at a school for developmentally disabled kids. One day, I had been crying all afternoon and was terribly upset, but I had been scheduled to supervise art projects with the kids. One of the students made a beeline for me as soon as I entered the room, and looked at me with a face so full of understanding and love that it really surprised me. Without saying a word, she placed her hand gently on the side of my face, looked into my eyes and nodded sympathetically. That simple gesture was the most comforting thing I had ever felt, and eroded the boundaries that existed between us.

I've thought about that young woman many times, and marveled at her ability to cut a swath directly to my heart. I long for the courage and directness she showed that day, and I long to see it on stage in improv scenes.

It has to start somewhere—why not with you and me? Silence offers room for human connection. When we look at each other the connection begins, and it leads us as far as we're willing to follow it. If we add touch into the mix—ooh, la la! *Now* we're talking about new improv territory. Why shouldn't we be the ones to chart it? All that's at stake is our old idea of the real world.

Notes

The Truth Right Now
Stimulus/Response Cycles

Everything that happens on stage should happen for a reason. If a character starts to cry, the audience wants to see the cause of that crying. If someone pulls a gun, we want to know what made him do it. Creating clear cause-and-effect on stage is simply a matter of responding to stimuli truthfully. In addition to exciting the audience, this has other benefits. Improv will be a whole lot simpler if you work with what's in front of you.

INSTINCTUAL RESPONSIVENESS

There's nothing more unexpected in this world than truthful human behavior, especially when the humans are in stimulus/response mode. Responding instinctually to a stimulus will bypass the conscious mind, and you'll find your responses are truer to the character and to the moment than ever before. If you are working off what your partner is *actually giving you*, the results will be both true and fresh.

Let's break this down into concrete examples. Two players are in a getting-a-divorce scene. The wife suddenly gets up and crosses the room. That's fine, so long as something happened to push her across the room. Perhaps sitting next to her husband

Everything that happens on stage should happen for a reason.

was too painful, so she is moving away from him. Perhaps she needs to feel air and space around her, so she is moving to comfort herself.

But what if, in a similar scene, the wife suddenly holds the husband and clings to him (even though she is instigating the divorce)? What possible motivation could she have to do that? Regret, ambivalence, longing for past partnership, sorrow, grief—there are a hundred believable reasons. Which choice is best? *Whichever one was predicated on the moment before.*

We do everything as the result of some stimulus, whether we know it or not. Have you ever found yourself saying something really odd and wondering why? Some need in you caused you to say that. Perhaps you needed to be thought witty, or you wanted to divert attention from a stain on your shirt — who knows? But *something* caused you to say it. Unfortunately, the stage is the only place where actions happen for no reason. And that's why life on the stage often looks so dead and unreal. Players are making "creative" choices for their actions that have no recognizable stimulus.

Let's look at how to respond truthfully at a very basic level. The following silent stimulus/response drill is adapted from an exercise in *The Empty Space* by Peter Brook.

Torso Fighting

Two players face each other and fight without touching. The hands, arms, head, legs and feet remain still; only the torso can move. Every blow must be given and received with vigor; the fighters must engage one another fully, with physical movements and emotional commitment. As you take a blow, receive it with the same force with which it was sent. Place your attention on receiving blows, reacting, and returning them to your partner.

As you continue the exercise, make your movements subtler. See how small the blows and responses can become, while retaining clarity about who is giving and who is receiving each blow. Pay attention to your focus. After the exercise, ask yourself what you noticed about your attention and focus as you made the movements subtler.

I'm fascinated by just how subtle the movements can become, and still the actors know who's giving and who's getting. The calmness and focus of this exercise is thrilling, as is the proof it offers about what instinctual creatures we are. Once we stop *performing* we can start *responding*.

Now that you've practiced physical cause-and-effect, try this exercise, which adds the elements of emotion and choice.

Stimulus/Response Exercise

This is a silent exercise. Stand facing a partner with your arms relaxed at your sides. You will play this exercise as yourself (not a character). You are not creating a narrative—you are responding as your actual self. Look at your partner and watch for any small movements, facial expressions, changes in breathing, etc. Let yourself respond naturally and without thinking to any changes you see in your partner. You're not mirroring, but responding. If your partner moves his neck and looks uncomfortable, you may instinctively want to reach out and rub it. Do it! If your partner looks at you and starts to laugh, and you don't understand why, respond as authentically as you can. This response may surprise you. While the typical thing to do would be to laugh along with him (even if you didn't feel like it), try to do what you feel like doing. Does his laughing at you make you feel uncomfortable? Then respond accordingly. Does his laughing make you mad? Respond in anger.

Don't do anything you don't genuinely feel like doing. Avoid being the wrong kind of polite. For instance, if your partner is playing make-believe hopscotch, and you don't want to, then don't. But remember, you must respond to everything your partner does; you're required to make use of the offer. Walk away, yawn, or steal his hopscotch rock—whatever feels most genuine to you.

Do the exercise for five or ten minutes. Avoid the urge to tell a story. This is simply a stimulus/response exercise to warm up and practice responding truthfully without speaking. It's easier to be honest when silent.

Being Affected vs. Pretending

It's important to make a distinction between being truly affected by your partner, and *adopting an affect*. In the first instance, you may feel caught off-guard and a bit surprised by your responses; in the second, you are staying safe and comfortable and *choosing* a response (which isn't necessarily connected to the stimulus that just occurred).

I'll give you an example from a scene I once saw. A father had called his daughter into the living room to talk to her. It was clear he was displeased about something. The improviser playing the daughter came into the room and instead of responding to the father's displeasure, she acted as though he was happy with her. She was unwilling to be uncomfortable, even though that would have been the most obvious state for her *character* to be in. This improviser made the scene more complicated by refusing to be affected by her partner.

The audience needs to see the origin of everything that happens on stage. They will not be satisfied with manufactured responses. To fulfill this obligation to our audience, we have to be willing to relinquish control—to our partners, to the story and to our emotions. Although we may resist giving up control at first, in the long run it can actually be quite relaxing, because when we give up control, we can stop feeling worried about the outcome of the scene. We begin to understand that our only responsibility is to give and take truthfully, and let fate decide the rest.

The audience needs to see the origin of everything that happens on stage.

The previous exercises were silent. Now you're going to add language. The trick here is to be as authentic and instantaneously responsive when you speak as you were when you were torso fighting. This requires breaking some old habits, because most improv conversation is shaped like this:

Player 1: TALK TALK TALK TALK TALK TALK TALK TALK TALK. [*Pause*]

Player 2: [*Pauses to be sure partner is finished*] TALK TALK TALK TALK TALK TALK TALK TALK TALK. [*Pause*]

Player 1: [*Pauses to be sure partner is finished*] TALK TALK TALK TALK TALK, etc.

Many a scene has died in those pauses because the improvisers weren't engaged in a genuine interaction. They were politely waiting for each other to finish every last thought before responding.

In the following exercise, the stakes go up, because you will not be improvising—you'll be speaking and reacting as yourself.

Interactions from Real Life

Two improvisers sit facing each other; the rest of the group will watch. The players have a conversation. They are not playing characters. This is not a performance; it's an exercise to practice listening and responding in a genuine way. One improviser says something to the other person. This might be something that happened to them that day, or something they've been thinking about. It's best if it's something fresh, and not an anecdote from ten years ago (unless the improviser has been thinking about that experience recently). It doesn't matter what the improviser talks about as long as it's real, and not a made-up narrative. The other player responds in whatever way she wants. If she's bored, she can say "So what?" or if she's interested she can say, "Really? That's interesting." The important thing is to respond genuinely, with no regard to social constraints.

Once the initial offer and response have been made, the improvisers should continue to talk like normal people. Like actual humans. This means interrupting each other when the impulse hits them, and not worrying about taking turns. Only actors take turns talking. In scripted theater, the constraints of the written dialogue shape the interaction, but in improv, we have the luxury of creating more believable speech patterns.

In real life, unless we're in a very formal setting, we interrupt each other a lot. Sometimes we only interrupt to make little "I'm listening" noises, or we shift our physical positions. Other times we break in to ask a question, or to exclaim "Me, too!" We may also interrupt in order to take over the conversation. This dynamic give-and-take is one of the keys to making stage conversation sound genuine.

There's another important reason to interrupt each other, and that is that at the moment you feel the urge to interrupt, you are at the peak of the stimulus/response cycle. In other words, your partner has said or done something that makes you want to respond *right now*. If you wait until your partner is done talking (which may take forever) and then respond, the peak of the moment has passed, and now your response is likely to be stale or even completely false. It's much better to interrupt each other at the moment we are compelled to do so; it will catch our partners off guard, and will give our interactions the quality of real, unpredictable exchanges.

By the way, this is true for all your impulses. Act on them *the second they hit you*. Even a good offer can hurt a scene if you sit on it and wait to embody it. Many "bad" offers are just good impulses that got stale—they would have been perfectly great if used at the moment they were conceived.

During the exercise, as soon as the improvisers are off and running, the content of the conversation can go anywhere. This is not about creating narrative. The focus should remain on responding to whatever your partner does (including shifts in body position, facial expressions, etc.). This exercise is a good way to get over being the wrong kind of polite, since the point is to respond to your own impulses and to express those impulses as clearly as possible.

It's very important to be genuine in this exercise. If your partner has said something you think is stupid, you should say so. Let the chips fall where they may. The whole point is to create a truthful interaction and see what happens. Obviously, this isn't about being mean or unkind. You wouldn't start an interaction by saying, "You're fat." It's simply about not avoiding your own reactions to things because you think they are unacceptable. It's also about calling your partner on behavior you think is false. If, for example, he says, "I love my job," and it's clear from his body language and voice that he's lying, you could say, "Really? It doesn't sound like it." The idea is for us to help each other see how often we gloss over the truth to make life smoother for ourselves. The foundation of theater is that life is uncomfortable and unpredictable, so the more we can give ourselves over to those qualities, the richer our scenes will be.

> *Act on your impulses the second they hit you. Offers have an expiration date; even a good offer will hurt a scene if it comes too late.*

The first few times you do the exercise you may behave too politely, in which case the exercise will have no life in it. Once you and your partner can get to truthful behavior, the exercise is usually very interesting to watch. Our ensemble has even used this exercise to start shows, and the audience response was very positive. The audience felt they got a glimpse inside the actors' heads before the improvising started, and they reported that it made the remainder of the show much more interesting. The improvisers (for the most part) liked the exercise, because their first activity in front of the audience was simply to be themselves—without the strain of having to maintain characters and create narrative.

As you watch the exercise, pay attention to which moments hold your interest and which moments seemed forced. For me, the most interesting moments are always those in which one or both players let their guard down and reveal something about themselves. These moments are often non-verbal or quasi-verbal. They may consist of the improviser shifting in the chair and making an emotional noise, accompanied by a relaxation of the muscles in the body. Those moments of relaxation signal that the improviser has stopped feeling self-conscious. Self-consciousness may return in the very next moment, but for that instant they were revealing themselves to us.

It's useful both to do and to watch this exercise because we need to learn what we feel like when we have allowed ourselves to be caught off guard. What causes those moments? Do they occur when we are so absorbed in what is being said (or in our reaction to it) that all our notions of being watched fall away? Do they happen when something strikes us as funny and we allow ourselves to laugh and to stop thinking for a minute? Do they happen when something angers us, or moves us, or intrigues us?

Yes, yes, and yes.

There are three reasons that we use our real lives for this exercise. The first is so that we don't have to spend any energy on thinking up a story. The second is that we are usually more invested in our real lives than in the fictitious lives we create on stage, and therefore tend to have stronger reactions, both in the telling and in the listening. Lastly, we are taking a bigger risk by talking about something true. We are more vulnerable and there's a greater likelihood that we'll be caught off-guard and reveal something about ourselves.

Listening and Responding to Intention

When we communicate, we use words, body language, vocal tone, facial expression, and emotion to convey our meaning. Words are perhaps the least important part of that mix. In fact, studies have shown that in communication, the listener takes 70 percent of meaning from the way the speaker looks, 20 percent from the way she sounds, and only 10 percent from the words themselves. In real life, we take in what someone says to us and try to factor in all the signals we're getting to determine their real meaning, especially if we feel that the other person isn't being entirely truthful.

In improv, actors often respond solely *to the words* they're hearing, paying little or no attention to the intent behind them. So much is missed and scenes suffer. If you respond only to words, you'll find yourself in a three-way battle between your intellect, your body and your gut. Our instinctual response is often to non-verbal cues. If you buck this basic truism when you improvise, you're going to have some very weird body language in scenes.

With any luck, you already saw this notion demonstrated in Interactions from Real Life (page 71). If the players were really tuned in to each other and responding truthfully, you probably saw some responses that were reactions to *subtext*, rather than the words being spoken. Here's an exercise designed to help you respond solely to intention.

Don't just respond to the words of your partner; start listening and responding to the intent BEHIND the words.

Subtext Ball

Players stand in a circle. The first player throws a space-object[5] ball to someone and says a line of dialogue. The player's intention (or subtext) must be very different from the words she is speaking. For example, she may say, "I hate you," but make it very clear with her body and voice that she is trying to seduce her partner. The partner then catches the ball and responds to her

---

5. A space object is an invisible object that the player mimes.

intention by saying something like, "I'll be over at eight o'clock!" This player then sends a new line of dialogue to another player, making sure that the subtext is very different from the words being spoken. For instance, he may say "I'm fine!" while conveying that he needs help or comfort. The responding player (who catches the ball) might say, "There, there, it'll be all right."

Play continues for several rounds, or until you can't think anymore. At first, this game is a bit of a brain fry. It may take you a few turns before it comes easily, but stick with it; it's great practice for responding to intention. It's also a good reminder that sometimes characters are lying.

UNCOVERING YOUR REAL RESPONSES

It's possible that you may be in an interaction and not know what your truthful reaction *is*. A number of factors could contribute to this. I often see it in people who are extremely polite in real life and who never interrupt anyone. These people may have been peacemakers in their families, they may have a cultural background that forbids interrupting, or they may be in professions that reinforce this behavior, such as counseling. I had one student who was a child psychologist, and he told me that in session he never says anything without thinking and must always choose his words very carefully, since they carry so much weight with his clients. This made improvising extremely difficult for him. Once he realized that improv was an arena where he could express himself openly (and without thinking), he began frolicking like crazy.

One way to uncover what we're really feeling is to use Primal Truths (page 24). In a scene, if your gut-level response to an offer is "I hate you," that's what you should say. Nothing more, and nothing *different*. Don't fancy it up. Don't water it down. Say "I hate you," leave room and see what happens.

One of the really great things about Primal Truths is that they are big, juicy, unmistakable offers to your partner. Said with conviction, there's no mistaking the meaning of "I hate you." Now the ball is in your partner's court to meet your challenge of honesty and emotionality in kind. Even if your partner isn't up to it, we will have had an electric moment in the scene that we will remember and savor.

Overcoming Defense Mechanisms

Feeling your emotional life stirring within you can be unsettling if you spend most of your time cut off from it. And if it stirs in front of a large, live audience, it can feel really threatening, causing your defense mechanisms to kick in. But you know what? Whether we like it or not, we have to be more courageous on stage than we are in real life. The first step to overcoming your defense mechanisms is to identify them.

Here's how *I* shut off on stage: by directing my partner, making him the protagonist, and making all the scary offers about *his* character. That way, the focus won't shift to me, and I won't be in danger of having to reveal my inner life. This is very insidious, because it looks extremely generous. In reality, I'm a big chicken. All these machinations ensure I won't have to feel anything in the scene. It has nothing to do with my partner really—it's simply my way of staying safe.

The antidote is tricky, because at first it feels uncomfortable. Practice being at risk in scenes. Speak in the "I" instead of the "you." For example, I'm in a scene playing a child who just got caught stealing. I might say, "I'm hungry," and as the actor, I have to fulfill that offer with truthful behavior. If instead I say, "You have plenty of food," that's not about my character—I'm trying to put the *other* actor on the spot. One choice is risky for me; the other is safe.

A common defense mechanism is what I call the Teflon Syndrome. Improvisers suffering from this malady are impervious to pain on stage, especially emotional pain. The Teflon player's wife says to him, "I want a divorce." The Teflon player says, "I was expecting as much," or "So what?" or "I've already filed for divorce." Anything to keep from taking the hit.

Don't let offers slide off you like eggs off a pan. Let them stick to you. Be affected. Let yourself be hurt, joyful, lustful, embarrassed, grief-stricken, panicked, or stupid. It's much more fun than being in control.

Some scenes require activities you simply don't know how to do. For instance, you may feel you can't do a French accent, or convincingly play a character from another time period. You may know nothing about nuclear physics or knitting. You're missing the point. The audience loves to see us do stuff we have no idea how to do. If we're more concerned with protecting our pride than we are with exploring the unknown, then the audience has a right to feel cheated. They aren't sitting out there in the dark to soothe our fragile egos—they want to see us knit (whatever we think that looks like) or do a lousy French accent (so they can feel superior knowing it's lousy.)

Part of the job of improvisers is to be cheerful about making fools of ourselves. The audience's appreciation of our work goes up in direct proportion to our willingness to play out of our depth. The further out on a limb we go, the better they like it. When you're out on that limb, make decisions quickly and act on them decisively. Tell the truth, even when it's imprudent to do so. Remember, these are stories; characters declare love, kill each other, climb mountains, and jump out of planes in numbers disproportionate to the general population.

Don't be afraid. Remember that you're jumping out of a *space-object plane*, you're declaring love to another *character*, and you're quitting a *pretend* job. There's no actual risk to you at all.

I saw a scene once where it was important to the story that the improviser kill a cat (I can't remember why). The improviser, a very kind-hearted woman, was stalling. I side-coached her as directly as I knew how: "Kill the cat," I said. She stalled some more, and still that cat was healthy. "Kill the cat," says I. She looked very distressed, until I said, "You know what? It's a space-object cat—it's OK to kill it." She was then able to kill it with abandon, and the scene was saved. It's sometimes helpful to remind ourselves that we're just pretending—it will lead to bolder choices and more decisive action.

Let's take another example. A man is applying for a job. As is sometimes the case in improv scenes, there is a special test he must pass to get the job—in this case, performing a striptease for his prospective boss. While many improvisers might avoid doing this, the player who is fun to watch will throw himself into it with everything he's got. After all, he's only going to pretend to take his clothes off. In a class, I saw a very funny example of this where once "naked," the improviser jumped around wildly and danced like a madman. Since we were picturing him nude, we could imagine his penis waving wildly in the air and the more he danced, the funnier the scene got.

> *The audience loves to see us do stuff we have no idea how to do.*

I don't remember the outcome of that scene, but I do remember thinking I would have hired him.

Stories don't have to follow everyday laws of logic, as long as they follow their own internal logic. In the example above, we didn't question *why* the employer demanded a striptease—it was part of the internal logic of the scene. So we were delighted when the striptease started, as it fulfilled the logic we had already accepted.

We often err on the side of being too conservative when we play. Almost any choice can fit into an internal logic system if we show the origin of the action, and play the choice with commitment. It's when we tippy-toe that we get into trouble.

Being Changed

Have you ever gotten the note, "You needed to change in that scene"? You might have thought that changing suddenly would look completely unrealistic to the audience. But if you allowed yourself to *be affected by stimuli continuously throughout the scene*, even a big change toward the end would seem natural.

Take sailboats for instance. Sailboats don't sail in a straight line. They zig and zag, continually affected by the wind. The sailor constantly adjusts the sail, moving it back and forth to catch even the slightest change in direction or intensity of the wind. These small, interactive movements cause the boat to move in the general direction the sailor wants to go, but the actual path is anything but straight.

The following exercise lets you experience being affected by your partner every single moment in a scene. Consider it sailing practice.

Even a 180° change will be believable if the audience has seen you shifting in response to stimuli throughout the scene.

Be Changed Round Robin

All players stand up, ready to jump into scenes quickly. Two players start a scene from nothing. One player (A) makes an offer of any kind: verbal, physical, emotional, etc. Player B is affected by the offer, and that response is his offer back to Player A. Now Player A is affected. Let the scene continue for a moment. The coach or other players should monitor the players on stage to ensure that they are changing slightly with each interaction. Often, a player will get stuck in one response mode for several interactions. It's helpful to point out what that stuck mode is, for example, "Joan, you've been angry for the last three exchanges. Listen to what he just said to you, and be affected by it."

The players shouldn't have to work to be affected. This isn't about manufacturing fake responses. It's about relaxing and being a human with another player.

It isn't necessary to finish the narrative of the scenes. After these two players have had a few moments to interact, two more players take their place. Play several rounds of the exercise to warm up the "be changed" muscle.

Scene Starts

Many improvisers find that the first moments of a scene are the hardest. At this point nothing has been established, we don't know who or what we are, and we stand on stage stripped of identity and purpose. Often our knee-jerk response to this (reinforced by our training, in many cases) is to start endowing like crazy. We endow our partners, our location, and ourselves with names, relationships and story elements. I believe we do this to feel more comfortable and safe. Once I (and my partner) know these elements, I can relax and worry less about making a mistake. But on a certain level, endowing is merely a way to control the scene and my partner.

When you first learned to improvise, you may have been very nervous about naming things, and your teachers probably had you play lots of endowment games to learn this important skill. Indeed, with beginning improvisers, scenes without endowments are usually quite boring, as the improvisers stand on stage and look nervous, or else talk aimlessly about nothing in particular. So it's good to know how to endow.

However, once you become more skilled, endowments can become the armor you wear to avoid being caught off-guard in those awkward moments on stage when you're unsure what's going on. Experienced improvisers often hit the stage with their guns blazing: "Hello, you're the president, I'm the press secretary. Here we are in the Oval Office." Well, how nice for everybody! God forbid we should establish relationships or characters and let the endowments emerge from the interaction! The challenge

Endowments can become the armor you wear to avoid being caught off-guard in those awkward moments when you're unsure what's going on.

is to *use* your natural confusion and the awkwardness you feel at the beginning of interactions to create engaging and organic scenes. Practicing truthful responsiveness in Interactions from Real Life can be the first step on this path. Once you become accustomed to picking up on even small signals from your partner and reacting from a gut level, you may find that you look forward to those electric moments of being off-balance, because they bring excitement and spontaneity to the stage.

As for endowments, I'm not advocating throwing the baby out with the bathwater. Nobody likes watching a scene that remains completely undefined. We need names, relationship and location information eventually. I'm suggesting that we let that information emerge *organically* in the course of the scene, after the first connecting moments with our partner have given us a base of truthful interaction from which to work. In this way we can avoid the urge to control by defining, and allow ourselves to experience being both off-balance and engaged with our partners.

Let information emerge organically in the course of the scene.

I'll give you an example of a delightful scene in which the improvisers had the courage to let information unfold in its own time. Two men were on stage; one was seated and relaxed, the other walking around tensely. In the first moments of the scene, we got to know each of them through the very strong character work they were doing. One character (Craig) was cheerful and easygoing and given to smiling a lot; the other (Goose) was high status and uptight and wanted to be in control. He blamed Craig for their predicament (as yet unnamed). Craig's whole goal in life seemed to be to get Goose to loosen up and have some fun. Goose, on the other hand, wanted Craig to admit his culpability and show some respect. It wasn't until well into the scene that we learned that they were in prison, sharing a cell. By the time that piece of information emerged, it was hysterically funny to the audience. If we had known at the beginning of the scene that it took place in prison, I'm sure the whole thing would have been quite different and, I'm convinced, far less satisfying. By engaging in a stimulus/response dance together, the actors watched the scene unfold along with the audience.

That dance is only possible when players are connected and paying attention to one another. The next time you're watching an improv scene, watch for the lowering of the isolation tanks. This usually happens right after an improviser gets the suggestion, and it looks like an invisible glass bell jar slamming down over each player until they are imprisoned in small isolation tanks. It can also happen in the middle of a scene. You know it's happening if the improvisers lower their eyes and start thinking. They have become little islands unto themselves.

The isolation tank is not our friend, for several reasons. The first and worst is that it cuts us off from our partners and immediately makes us feel alone onstage. Second, it cuts us off from the moment at hand and causes us to miss the opportunity to start scenes from an organic place. Third, after emerging from the isolation tank, improvisers tend to look stiff and artificial, as they are now STARTING THE SCENE, which usually has a false look and feel. It would be much better to find the scene from the present moment. Don't take a personal time-out while you think up something to say.

Instead of lowering the bell jar over your head as a scene begins, keep your eyes up, look into your partner's eyes, watch his body, feel your own body, and breathe. Now you're ready to catch even the smallest first offer from yourself or your partner: a cough, an adjustment of clothing, a shifting of weight or subtle repositioning of the group. Scenes beginning this way delight the audience because they have seen the origin of the scene, and that makes them feel clever and observant.

Truthful responsiveness doesn't fall out of the sky like airplane parts. It's a skill you build over time; courage is required, as is the understanding that you're going to look like a big dope once in awhile. If you're fixated on looking intelligent or cool, you will never realize your full potential as an improviser. To respond truthfully, you must be willing to be connected not only to your partner, but also to yourself.

Real responses happen in real time and that time is measured in milliseconds. Imagine I just grabbed your face with both hands and gave you a big, sloppy kiss on the mouth. Do you:

a. stop and think about what I've done, sort through possible responses and choose the one you think the audience will like best?

b. slap me?
c. laugh in my face?
d. kiss me back?

The correct answer is: b, c, or d, depending on how you felt when I kissed you. It really is just that simple. Six million improv rules won't help you now. This is about you, me, and two sets of lips. That's all it's about. And believe me, that's plenty.

Finding the Shiny Thing
Seeking Pleasure

Imagine wallowing in pleasure. Maybe it's a vat of chocolate, or that kiss I just gave you, or lying on a beach, or listening to music. Close your eyes for a moment and breathe in the pleasure of that moment. Let it flood your body.

Now imagine the way you feel when you're improvising. Is it the same feeling? Is your body as gooily relaxed? Are your nerve endings stimulated?

Pleasuring yourself on stage is not only the secret to improvising. It's also the only reason to do it in the first place. Look, there's precious little money to be made in improv, so you'd better invent your own payoff every time you step on stage. Create your own fun; what *you* think is fun, not what the guy next to you thinks. The Shiny Thing is another term for your unique and peculiar notions of pleasure.

Our bodies and minds follow our genuine interests—if we let them. The Shiny Thing is anything that happens in a scene that catches the fancy of one of the improvisers. It's a bit tricky to talk about, because it can take any form. I'll try to explain it and then give you some examples I've seen.

The Shiny Thing can be any aspect of an interaction, character trait, physical object, or offer that sparks a reaction in you.

Imagine wallowing in pleasure every time you step on stage.

The metaphor is a shiny little ball that hovers in the air, catching the light. You want to follow the little ball the way a bird looks at its reflection in a mirror. And you play with your Shiny Thing as long as it interests you, dropping it when you've played out your interest.

One example of this: an improviser was playing an Italian man talking to an American woman with whom he'd had a brief fling some months before. When she turns up at his apartment to retrieve a book she left there, he starts looking for the book. In the course of the search, they are chatting, and as he goes to a space-object cupboard, he tries to think of the English word for it. She says "cupboard" and he says, "No, that is not what I am thinking of." She tries "bookshelf?" He responds, "No, another word, I think." She tries a few more ideas, and he replies with a smile, "Now you are just fooling with me." They leave the cupboard and the conversation turns elsewhere, but later in the scene, he returns to the cupboard, pats it gently and says, almost to himself, "What word is this called?" By now the audience was howling, because the improviser was so invested in what interested him, namely, that cupboard. He didn't ignore his partner, but he was following his *own* interests, too. He was having a fine time playing with that cupboard.

On the page, there's nothing hysterically funny about that example. It was the delight with which the improviser engaged the moment that made it work. And, lest you think that he hijacked the scene, or ground it to a halt, far from it. His character's obsession with being correct and always having the upper hand became central to the narrative—it became part of the explanation for why the couple had not stayed together.

In another scene, one improviser, Christopher, was playing a desk clerk with another improviser, Kurt. The first time the clerk stepped up to the desk to help Kurt, he placed both his palms face down on the desk and leaned far over it, with a helpful look on his face. "May I help you?" he said while in this position. Whenever Kurt spoke, Christopher withdrew his hands and pulled away from the desk, dropping his arms to his sides and lowering his eyes shyly. This meant that whenever Kurt was speaking, there was no eye contact. In other words, Christopher was just messing with Kurt's head. His character *seemed* intent on providing good service, because he was so enthusiastically involved whenever he himself spoke; it was when he was silent that his character disengaged and became aloof. Again, this scene was so funny that we almost peed ourselves; half the humor came from Kurt trying to find new ways to get Christopher to really listen to him and help him with his needs. Kurt was having a hard time not laughing because Christopher's behavior was so outlandish. So in this case, Christopher's Shiny Thing drove *Kurt's* choices, and gave Kurt a lot to work with in terms of his objective.

Shiny Things can be discovered when you're playing small roles, too. I once saw a café scene in which the waiter (an intermittent supporting character) was very slow and precise with his movements. It didn't have anything to do with the main story line, but it rounded out the action of the scene, because it took him forever to get to the table with his slow, measured steps. He walked in very straight lines, always retracing his steps to and from the kitchen. The improviser didn't pull focus with this bit, but was having a very good time with his Shiny Thing.

A few caveats are worth mentioning. Shiny Things *can* pull focus if they're used indiscriminately or with disregard to the main action. The purpose of a Shiny Thing is not to be self-indulgent at the expense of the scene, but to learn to find joy and amusement by following your true interests. To be useful, a Shiny Thing must occur organically—it can't be forced. It's not a matter of starting a scene in Shiny Thing overdrive, but more about having your antennae up to catch the slightest blip on your radar screen. Now that I've violated the Maximum Metaphor Law, let me say that another way.

During scenes, any number of offers or incidents may strike our fancy (causing the first big blip on the radar screen), but we often ignore these or push them away, thinking that they don't have anything to do with the main action. The audience sees our response to everything, and they note whether we follow our instincts or not. In a scene where there is only one jelly doughnut left on the plate, the audience will see if one character's eyes wander over to the plate. If they do, the audience then wants to see some result of that interest—like diving for the doughnut. If the improviser squashes this impulse, the audience has been cheated. They feel the interest surge at the same time we do; we are fulfilling the audience's wishes when we pay attention to those surges and follow them up with action.

Remember, the audience sees everything that happens in a scene. When we experience an interest surge, so do they.

I love the following two Shiny-Thing-inspired exercises for opening up our fun channels.

Mr. Bean Solos and Scenes

Rowan Atkinson, the brilliant British comic actor, has created a character called Mr. Bean. Mr. Bean dances with the minutiae of everyday living like Fred danced with Ginger. No activity is rushed; changing clothes for a swim at the beach can take ten minutes. It's not that Mr. Bean is having fun, exactly (although Rowan Atkinson certainly is). It's that each small step in life gets fully executed. So, for instance, Mr. Bean drops his pencil on the floor while taking a test. He first looks around to see if anyone noticed him dropping the pencil. Then he looks at the pencil, fixing its precise location with his eyes; he then looks around (to see if anyone is watching) and slowly begins to lean over toward the pencil. He is obviously trying very hard to remain unnoticed. At this point his chair creaks. He freezes. He may slowly sit back up and start the whole procedure again. Or he may continue leaning down and bump his head on the desk. And so on.

Mr. Bean is one big Shiny Thing because he is affected by everything in his environment, and he is buffeted emotionally by every tiny choice he makes.

Mr. Bean Shiny Thing Practice

Each player will do a silent, solo scene. Get a suggestion or start from nothing. The first thing the player does (laughs, coughs, shifts in her chair, looks out a window) forms the basis of the scene. Pay attention to your environment. Let what's happening have an emotional effect on you. See how many tiny, incremental parts are contained in a seemingly simple few moments on stage. Enjoy the way your body feels when you're using it fully. Elasticize your face. Exaggerate life.

After you've all had a chance to do a Mr. Bean solo, pair up and play interactions with your partner. Keep the interactions silent so you can concentrate on the joy of physicality and emotion. Watch where your genuine interests lead you—and follow them.

Monty Python Scenes

Another way to raise your pleasure antennae is to do improvised scenes in the style of Monty Python. These gentlemen were not known for their great narrative; what drove their scenes was the absurd level of investment in interactions both mundane and ridiculous.

Python Practice

With your fellow players, perform some improvised scenes in the style of Monty Python. If you're unfamiliar with Monty Python, I urge you to rent videos of their 1960s series. Look for these general conditions:

- characters are very invested in getting what they want
- they do not observe rules of customary behavior
- everyone reacts to every offer
- extreme emotion is the norm
- scenes may be intercut with other scenes, especially if the first scene is failing
- time and place are flexible notions; a scene from the Spanish Inquisition might well include modern-day characters
- interrupting is allowed (encouraged, even)
- authority figures are often played absurdly
- characters talk in funny British accents
- men play women

If you're getting a sense from reading this list that anything goes, you're exactly right. Do whatever you want in the scenes. Listen to what your partners are saying, and respond as primitively as possible, with big gestures, loud, confident remarks, and overblown emotions. Run around the stage, shout and pursue your objectives. Don't worry about the narrative. The main focus is on responding heartily to everything that happens—to not let any offer pass unnoticed. In Monty

> Python scenes, everything is important; characters are not blasé about anything, unless the choice of being blasé is itself blasphemous or unexpected.

Oddly enough, Monty Python scenes can also be very helpful for group scenes, because they give us the chance to practice listening to others and being invested in our own business at the same time. I've noticed that Monty Python scenes often have more clarity and focus than more subdued group scenes. They seem to foster a heightened sense of attentiveness in the improvisers. I believe that's because improvisers are playing with more emotional abandon, and are therefore keenly interested in everything that happens on stage.

FINDING YOUR OWN FUN

To practice finding Shiny Things, set aside some special rehearsals to explore them. Make an agreement with your fellow players that you aren't going to worry about narrative at all, and that each of you will be paying attention to following your impulses and interests in scenes. It may be that some scenes have no Shiny Things in them; it may be that some players are better at this than others. Don't get all in a twist about it, or you'll subvert the whole idea.

Underneath your clothes you'll find a fully operational, self-contained amusement park. Inside your head, behind the dented, cobwebbed cans of duty, worry, and regret are racks and racks of your favorite pleasures. Pluck those pleasures when you improvise. Play your own music in scenes. Have fun before the lights go out.

Forget about the story for now. Focus on your own pleasure.

Part Two

Nuts and Bolts

Notes

Whose Journey Is It?
Protagonist-Centered Storytelling

There are a lot of viewpoints on what makes good narrative structure in improv, and some people would argue that any structure at all is antithetical to the nature of improv itself. I know how freewheeling improv is—that's why I love it, too. But I've been in too many scenes where everyone is flailing around, without a clue of who the scene's about, or *what* it's about, and it seems useful to try to get a grip. Somehow. A great way to start is to have a central character.

Having watched hundreds of improv scenes over the past several years, I'd have to say that most of them don't have a clear-cut protagonist who stays the protagonist throughout the scene. Far more common is a scene centering around first one character, then another, then another, until finally, blessedly—the lights come down.

In protagonist-centered narrative structure, there is a central figure (the hero) whose story is followed. Ideally, the hero's journey will be one worthy of our involvement. With luck, our hero will have a goal that seems beyond her reach, will come up against obstacles (both internal and external), will overcome those obstacles, and in the process, gain self-knowledge, and will in the end be changed by the whole endeavor. Heroes' journeys can range from epic quests to the small, everyday challenges of being human.

This structure requires that all the players know who the story is about, and that everyone strives to ensure the story *remains* centered on that character. You'll need extraordinary attention skills and a rare degree of selflessness. To create hero-centered scenes, try these steps:

1. Establish the protagonist
2. Define the journey (which involves posing a question to which we want to know the answer)
3. Raise the stakes and develop the scene
4. Answer the question definitively
5. Show how the protagonist has been changed

An important note: don't look on these as hard-and-fast rules. This narrative structure is intended as a way to help you practice the concept of hero-centered journeys. The idea is not that everyone on stage should be keeping a checklist, looking ahead and making arbitrary choices. Rather, the hope is that this will deepen your understanding of narrative, and help you recognize where you are at any given point in a story. Like any improv theory, you should practice it in rehearsal and put it on the back burner for performance.

And since we've stopped at the side of the road, here's another tidbit: protagonist-centered stories work for both short scenes and long forms. In a long form, each of the steps can be explored in more depth and detail. But even short scenes will benefit from having a focused hero's story.

1. Establish the Protagonist

The protagonist is often an Everyman character who serves as a surrogate for the audience. The audience says, "I can see myself in that situation," and then delights in having a second-hand experience, without all the emotional wear and tear. If the scene has established this kind of Everyman, remember that to keep the audience's interest and faith in you, your character must behave in a way that commands their loyalty. The audience is rooting for you, and you must play characters for whom

If you're playing an Everyman protagonist, your character should behave in a way that commands the audience's loyalty.

we are happy to root. This is one of the best reasons I know to steer away from protagonists who are rude, controlling, or nasty. (It's *possible* for such a person to be the protagonist, a difficult feat we will look at later.) Also, be careful if you tend to play high status all the time; high-status characters are rarely the heroes in stories.

The audience likes to imagine itself in the best possible light: trustworthy, intelligent, sensitive, etc. Therefore, if you topple their illusions about themselves by having their surrogate behave boorishly, you will probably lose their loyalty as well as their interest.

The protagonist in the story is the person who has the most at stake. Keith Johnstone quotes a definition of "hero" that suits perfectly: "The hero is the one who suffers for a worthwhile cause." The cause must be worthy, or our interest in the hero will be slight. And if we're not intrinsically interested in the hero, our attention will wander, causing the improvisers to start waving their arms and shouting.

So how do you actually figure out who the protagonist is? It's not a matter of deciding ahead of time who will be the protagonist, or artificially imposing it on someone. Rather it's about paying close attention to the first few offers—verbal and non-verbal—and seeing what emerges naturally. Someone's body movement may be an offer in and of itself. In a group scene, the physical positions of the actors may identify the protagonist. Be watching. Be ready. This is where being present in your body and in the moment will be especially useful. Watch with big eyes. Have your antennae fully extended for even the smallest nuance that will start the story.

Ideally, one character will stand out by having a strong emotional reaction to something early on, or we'll get an important piece of information ("Rebecca, this is your last chance in the Olympics") or some other clue that lets us know "*This* is the story I will be following."

We will make the hero someone with whom the audience can identify, and make the struggle he faces worthwhile. The classic themes are worth revisiting: love, power, pride, greed, lust, fear. These continue to strike chords in us for good reason. So if your hero is trying to get a job at McDonald's, the underlying reason should be more compelling: maybe the young man is trying to prove himself worthy of trust, for instance.

> *The protagonist in the story is the person who has the most at stake.*

> *Determine the protagonist by paying close attention to the first few offers and seeing what emerges naturally.*

We'll care a lot more about his success or failure if we understand that.

By definition, the protagonist must respond emotionally to the situation at hand. The goal must be something she longs for with all her heart. Ambivalence is death in improv. The *obstacles* should have an effect on her, too. At every step of the way, the audience should be able to identify with the struggle. The audience may have information the character doesn't have, which can be interesting. For instance, the audience may see that the hero's fear is going to hold her back from succeeding at public speaking. That only enhances our appreciation of the scene.

In the opening moments of the scene, the first improviser to be emotionally or personally at risk is usually the protagonist. If the ensuing story centers on this person, we're off to an excellent start.

When practicing the skill of identifying the hero, pay attention to who is doing the defining. It's often the *other characters* in the scene (this is like shouting "Not it!" in a game of tag). I've noticed this tendency a lot. I think it's about our wanting to be in control, but it goes deeper than that. On some level, we know the hero is going to go on a journey (scary right off the bat), and that he will be put through emotional experiences (scarier still) and that if all goes well, he will be changed by the experience (who's lining up to have that happen to them?). So, we take the safe role, the non-vulnerable role, of not-the-protagonist.

If you see this tendency in your own work, try establishing yourself as the protagonist once in awhile. To do this, speak in the "I." For example, instead of saying to another player, "Boy, you're going to be in so much trouble with the boss," say, "Boy, *I'm* going to be in so much trouble with the boss." That way, instead of trying to force the protagonist role on your partner, you are shouldering it yourself. Similarly, phrases like "I'm afraid," "I can't do that," "I want this more than anything in the world," signal to the audience that you will be the hero in our story. It may seem at first glance that establishing yourself as the protagonist is hogging all the action, but as noted above, most people are fairly reluctant to be the protagonist when they are just starting out. Hey, somebody's got to do it. It might as well be you.

To play the non-protagonist (which isn't necessarily an *antagonist*), the improviser should be less emotionally affected

Ambivalence is death in improv.

If you're always endowing someone else as being the protagonist, try speaking in the "I."

by the circumstances. The non-protagonist has less to lose or gain by the outcome of the story. Any time an improviser other than the hero has a strong emotional reaction, it should *feed into the hero's story*, not sidetrack the story onto another path. I call this hijacking the protagonist's role. The way hijacking usually works is this: let's say we have a scene in which the husband in the story is our protagonist, and he's afraid that his wife is going to leave him. As he talks to his wife about his fears and his love for her, if she starts being more emotionally invested than he is, she will start stealing the "hero focus." She may also put out new information to make her character more sympathetic, such as "I just learned I have cancer," which will confuse the issue mightily.

If you're not the protagonist, beware of hijacking the story.

This often happens when the other character in the scene isn't comfortable being the bad guy. One of the great things about protagonist-centered storytelling is that everyone can play their roles with complete abandon, because they know they're serving the central story. So, if the actor is called upon to be the wife, she should be as unsympathetic as possible, knowing that her actions will only make us root harder for the protagonist.

Protagonist Round Robin

The best way to learn to identify the protagonist is to practice starting scenes. Here's a simple exercise. Two players start a scene. One player makes an offer and the other player accepts the offer. They continue until someone watching thinks the protagonist has been established and yells "Freeze." Then both players in the scene point to the protagonist. One thing to remember about establishing the protagonist (and calling, "Freeze"): everyone on stage needs to be in agreement about who the hero is. It isn't enough for one player to endow the other as the hero. The second player must accept the endowment, and make his acceptance clear to everyone on stage. For example, Player A may say, "So, you're up for that big promotion today." Player B would accept this hero endowment by saying, "Yes. I'm so nervous, I'm afraid I'm going to blow the interview." If this is said with emotional enthusiasm, we now have our protagonist.

The most common occurrence when improvisers first play this game is that they will Ping-Pong their hero offers. Player A will say, "So, you're up for that big promotion today," and Player B will respond, "Yes, and I hear you're going to be fired." Who's the protagonist? Nobody so far. If this happens and Player A is savvy enough, he will reply, "Oh my God—I am? I can't lose my job—I have a family to support." Now Player A is our hero and Player B missed his chance. *Until both players know who the protagonist is, we can't proceed with the rest of the story.*

It's much easier to see who the hero is when you're standing outside the scene. Therefore, when you are just beginning to play this game, the players watching the scene should be quiet and let the actors do the pointing. If the actors in the scene have no idea who it is, then the audience can help them.

Besides pointing to the hero, it's important that the actors state the reason(s) he is the protagonist. Sometimes there will be differences of opinion about who the protagonist is, and there may be more than one possibility, especially if everyone on stage is reacting with emotion to the offers being made. (This is an excellent problem to have. If you get to the point where everyone in your ensemble is always reacting with emotional commitment to every offer, please call me so I can drink some champagne.) The way to handle this is to remember that the *first* person to have a big emotional response to the situation is our hero. All subsequent emotional offers by other characters should be a bit scaled back, with the exception of a villain, who can play as robustly as he wishes.

The first person to have a big emotional response to the situation is our hero.

When playing Protagonist Round Robin, make sure to vary who is endowing whom with the role of hero. Sometimes the protagonist can endow herself, and sometimes the endowment can come from other players. You should become adept at both approaches.

2. Define the Journey: Pose the Question of the Story

So now we have a hero. We're going to send him out for a set of experiences (the journey) that will change him—and us, if we're lucky. The hero's journey should be important or we won't be interested. It's that simple. Even if the story seems inconsequential on the surface, if it's important enough to the hero, we as the audience will find it important, too.

Speaking of the audience, they often see the question of the scene before we do. It's lovely, then, to define the story that they have already hoped to see. *Do this by paying attention to the first offers in the scene, no matter how small.* The first interaction establishing relationship often suggests the journey that will follow. For example, if a scene begins with a tense father/son relationship, the question of the scene may be, "Will the son gain the father's respect?"

If the question seems inconsequential, such as, "Will he get the job?" then the players must raise the stakes for the hero: e.g., his family is starving. All the improvisers on stage should be making the journey important.

I find that most unsuccessful improv scenes go awry in the first few moments. Either the protagonist is not clearly established, or else the question of the scene is muddy. The journey usually involves some aspect of *relationship*: the hero in relation to another person, to herself, or to the world. Here are some examples that arise in literature, film, and plays:

- will they stay together or break apart?
- will the parent accept the child?
- will the hero grow into the role she finds herself in (queen, wife, boss, or adventurer)?
- will the innocent's voice be heard?
- will evil triumph?
- does human nature ever change?

Where these themes are often *not* explored (or not explored in enough depth) is in improv. I suspect it's because they're deep, scary, primal themes that send us scurrying for cover. And, as my friend Doug Nunn pointed out, they're highly complex. In the comfort of a play, where we know the outcome, and we know what happens to our character, we are more willing to explore them. But in improv, where we *can't* know the outcome, it takes a lot more courage and a keen ability to pay attention.

How do you pose the question of the scene? As clearly as possible. It's great to say (as the father in a father/son scene):

"You'll never amount to anything." Or, if you're the Olympic coach, say to the athlete, "No woman has ever broken the four-minute mile." Muddier versions of the above offers might include (father to son): "You drive me nuts, coming in here and moping around and acting like the world owes you something." This sounds on the surface like a strong offer because it might stimulate strong emotions in the son, but it doesn't pose the question of the scene. It doesn't define the journey. In the coach/athlete scene, this offer might occur: "There's a lot at stake here. You've trained hard. The other runners look strong today." This offer hints at the question, but doesn't give us a sense of importance beyond the context of this race. When making the offer that defines the journey, the more overtly and simply stated the better. Don't be fancy. Don't be oblique. Be straightforward, and state the question with feeling.

Define the journey simply and clearly.

Someday, when we are all skilled in these techniques and can do them in our sleep, maybe then we can be more Pinteresque with our offers. Until then, *be simple and direct.*

One more thought about the journey. There isn't a "right" one for any particular scene. Any one of a number of journeys may be plausible within the given circumstances. Just pick one and make it obvious. Once the question of the scene is clear, the next skill is in keeping it on track, and not wandering off into the woods. That's what the next step is all about. But first, a way to practice defining the journey.

Protagonist Round Robin 2 – Pose the Question

Players play the game as before, except this time the scene will continue until both the protagonist and the journey (question of the scene) have been defined, at which point a player watching will say "Freeze." After the freeze is called, the players on stage point to the protagonist, and state the question of the scene. Again, there might be some disagreement about the question of the scene. If neither player has any clue what the question is, they should resume play and try to clarify the question in the next few exchanges. Players on the sidelines should avoid helping unless the whole thing deteriorates and people are starting to get grumpy.

In the father/son example, the question of the scene ("Will he gain his father's respect?") was raised at the same time the protagonist was established. It's often the case that when a player accepts the hero endowment cleanly and clearly, the question will be raised simultaneously. Here's another example: a group of girls is standing on stage. One improviser says, "Show the new postulant into Reverend Mother's office." One player steps forward; the girl next to her says, "How can you be so sure about your calling?" And the postulant replies, "That's what I'm here to find out." Boom! Clean and clear, we have a hero and her journey in one fell swoop.

Well done! However, in most scenes we won't have such a delicious double play, so the journey will be defined in a separate offer.

Let's say we have a scene in which all the kids at school are picking on the fat girl. Player A has accepted the endowment of being the fat girl, but we still don't know what her journey will be. At that point, someone in the scene (either Player A or another player) should make a clear "journey" offer, such as, "I know you have a crush on Tommy, but he's out of your league." Or her mother might say, "You have to learn to love yourself, no matter what other people think of you." This second offer is actually stronger, because the outcome of the journey rests solely on the shoulders of the protagonist. The Tommy offer may take away the protagonist's ability to participate in the outcome of her own story: she will be waiting for Tommy to decide if he likes her.

Offers that rely on other characters' actions may lead to scenes in which the protagonist is just moved around the story like a prop; it's far more satisfying for the journey to require real involvement on the part of the hero. So, to use another example, if we have a scene in which our hero is very shy and afraid to speak in public, it would be better if the question of the scene is: "Will she overcome her fear and speak at the rally?" than "Will the principal give her an award?" We want to watch our heroes take action to achieve their goals. We don't want them to sit around hoping another character will do their hard work for them.

Our heroes represent our ideal vision of ourselves; we want them to go after their dreams with the kind of vigor we can't always muster.

The protagonist's actions should contribute the main movement in the story. Beware of scenes where everyone else is moving the hero around like a prop.

3. Raise the Stakes and Develop the Scene

Besides knowing what the hero is pursuing, we must understand why it is important to him. We must also know the consequences of failure. After the hero and his journey are identified, all the subsequent offers should serve the same purpose: to deepen and enrich the journey. Other characters can and should emerge, other information should be given about the hero and the circumstances, BUT they should all feed into the main story—the journey of the hero. To raise the stakes, first we add to what we already know by discovering:

- why the journey is important to her
- the consequences of failure

Once we know who the hero is, we must understand the risks of the journey and the consequences of failure.

Once these elements have been established, we can turn up the heat under the protagonist and make the journey, and its outcome, more important. At this stage, we will:

- pose obstacles to success
- deepen the consequences
- tie other lives to the protagonist's life

For instance, if our hero has been wrongly thrown in jail, we can raise the stakes by introducing the violent cellmate, seeing a corrupt cop destroy evidence and/or meeting the hero's ailing mother.

In this step of raising the stakes, it's terrific if the very obstacles themselves are somehow connected to the consequences of success or failure. For example, in the father/son scene, one of the obstacles to the son may be the father's cold emotional state. If the son is trying to get his father to be more open because the father is a heart attack candidate, the obstacle and outcome of the journey are intertwined.

The obstacles, too, must have an emotional effect on the protagonist.

Like all important elements in the scene, the obstacles should have an emotional effect on the protagonist. At every step of the way, the audience should be able to identify with the hero's struggle. (I heard a great quote from the film director Arthur Penn: "A character is defined not by what he is able to do, but by what he is *unable* to do. That's why *Hamlet* is four hours long.") At times, the audience may have information the character doesn't have. For instance, the audience may see the cop destroying evidence, but the hero doesn't. That enhances our appreciation of the scene, and whets our appetites to see what happens.

When overcoming obstacles, it's very satisfying if the hero can muster personal qualities he didn't know he possessed. Looking again at our father/son scene, let's assume the son has never before been able to be honest with his father about his emotions. Let's further assume that he finds the inner strength to do so this time. In a wonderful improv world, the other improviser would be touched and changed by this unexpected strength and honesty from the hero.

Heroic quests are defined by the hero choosing a difficult path or solution, often at great cost to herself. That choice should ideally be rewarded, and in most good storytelling, it is. It is possible to have a good story where such behavior is not rewarded, but the balance is tricky.

A side note: I'm often hearing examples from my students about great books with unsympathetic heroes, compelling films with no protagonist at all, etc. Of course there are examples like these in literature, film and theater; each of those was the result of painstaking effort on the part of a writer, who toiled (sometimes for years) to make it work. My contention is that in improv, where all our impulses are secret until we manifest them with each other, it's best not to get too fancy with the form until we have it down cold. Then, by all means, go crazy. It's pretty rare to see a really compelling, rich story in an improv scene that didn't seem like a lucky accident. My goal here is to help make good storytelling the norm.

Relationships with Teeth

Back to scene development. In the heart of the scene, the relationships should be deepened and clarified. This includes ancillary relationships of other characters besides the main two or three. Again, the relationships should be developed in a way that *serves the main story*. Being clear and simple helps here, too. If in our well-thumbed father/son scene, the mother is another prominent character (either as helpful cheerleader, shrinking violet, or any other incarnation of Mother), her additions to the scene should either further the journey, up the stakes, or ideally, both.

When we talk about defining relationships we usually mean naming ourselves and our relationship to our partners ("Hi, Mom, I'm home from school.") While this is fine as far as it goes, it doesn't go far enough. In addition to knowing that the other actor is my mother, I should also let the audience know how I feel about her—what is the *nature* of our relationship? Benign? Friendly? Antagonistic? Competitive? There's no such thing as a neutral relationship, at least not in theater. Yet a lot of improv scenes involve people in carefully neutral relationships. Improv is more difficult when relationships are ill-defined. The more emotional history you have with another character, the simpler it is to interact.

By creating vibrant relationships, we open ourselves up to the possibility of being deeply affected by the other characters in the scene. This is especially crucial in protagonist-centered storytelling. If my relationship with my mother is competitive, then telling her I've gotten straight A's on my report card is suddenly a lot more important than if we have a benign and supportive relationship. If our relationship is benign and supportive, a stronger choice might be that I got straight D's, because it has the potential to challenge the status quo. In this way relationship can inform our narrative choices, as well as enhancing and deepening the scene.

Merely naming a relationship isn't enough. You must also define the NATURE of the relationship, so we can see its effect on the protagonist.

Raising the Stakes

The stakes are raised in a fictitious scene the same way they are in life. Information gets presented that casts a new light on the story. For instance, in our father/son scene, the stakes may be raised because the son is moving to Europe and knows he won't be returning home. The family may be in dire financial straits, and it's up to the son to take the reins. We may discover that the father beat the son regularly when he was a child. Any of these choices will raise our interest in the outcome of the story.

Another example of stake raising: a worker is struggling to finish an annual report to meet a deadline. He gets a ton of new information to include and discovers that his boss has been embezzling. Then the boss threatens to fire him if he doesn't hide the embezzlement. The question of the scene has deepened from "Will he get the report finished on time?" to "How will he handle the moral dilemma, and what will be the consequences?"

Making the consequences/rewards clear was touched on earlier. If we know that being fired would devastate the worker, we will be more invested in the outcome of the story. If he's ambivalent, we won't care much either.

Introducing Other Characters

In addition to raising the stakes, this is the point in the story where we may meet new characters. These characters should serve the purpose of deepening the story, preferably without adding a ton of new information. We may meet helpers and friends at this stage; villains may appear, and/or bystanders who simply help push the story forward.

Develop the Scene/Raise the Stakes

Two players get up and the group decides (arbitrarily) who the protagonist is, and invents the question of the scene. The players then begin playing the scene as if it had been going on already, and they focus on raising the stakes of the journey. New characters may be introduced, obstacles raised, etc. Don't worry about answering the question of the scene at this point—that's coming in a minute. This is a way to practice the middle of scenes, and this step is the one in which the players can wallow a bit, developing the characters more deeply, exploring relationships, and increasing our interest in the outcome of the scene.

All characters in the scene should be serving to deepen and clarify the protagonist's story.

4. Answer the Question Definitively

It's almost comical how difficult this step is for us. I can't tell you how many scenes I've watched or been in where the answer was avoided at all costs, even if it was self-evident. I think it comes from an erroneous idea that if we answer the question, the story is over. It isn't, as we'll see in a moment. A sort of slow motion, *Chariots of Fire* thing sets in at the end of scenes, too—a momentum problem that is easily addressed. If it's clear where the scene is headed, if you know it, the audience knows it, the stage manager knows it, for heaven's sake, just get there ASAP. There are several reasons for this, all of which are important:

If the audience can see where the scene is going, just get there as quickly as possible.

- the audience will feel clever that they "saw" the ending first
- no new information is being added; the interest lies in your ability to engage or move the audience by the way the story plays itself out (especially in regard to the effect on the hero)
- the end of a scene is no time to start doggin' it

Avoid Negotiating

The most common method of stalling the ending is negotiating. The loser of the outcome (usually the non-protagonist) wants to win at least a little bit, and tries to dilute the win of the hero by negotiating at the last minute. In the father/son scene, the father may start to embrace the son, then pull back and say, "You've got to admit, you aren't easy to love" or "I'd approve of you—IF . . ." This is negotiating, and it weakens the ending of stories. If the improviser playing the father can summon up the courage, he should simply embrace the son and say, "I love you." Or, "I'm sorry." The audience will fill in the rationale if the actors commit to the moment.

Avoid negotiating. It leads to a lot of excess conversation and dilutes the audience's response to the outcome of the story.

In the annual report scene, let's say the worker chooses the high road, exposes the embezzlement, and presents a brilliant report. Let's further say that the board of directors commends him. Now, nine times out of ten, at this point, the actor playing the boss will try to get the worker fired, or try to worm his way back into the good graces of the board. This muddles up the end of the story. Yes, it's more realistic. But it's not theatrical. Not only does negotiating lead to a lot of pointless extra conversation (which we have to get through before we can find out how the hero has been changed), but it dilutes the audience's response to the story. If they're yelling "Yahoo! The hero won!", don't spoil the party by saying, in effect, "Well— not just *yet.*"

Remember: TAKE THE WIN.

Negotiating sometimes comes from the protagonist too, which I find quite surprising, but there you are. This comes under the heading of "sore winner," and is very unappealing when it happens. Let's use the father/son scene again. If the father capitulates completely, falling into his son's arms and saying, "I've been a terrible father. Please forgive me. I love you so much" (I can dream, can't I?)—then the son should say, "I love you too, Dad. I'm so happy," or words to that effect. What the son shouldn't say is, "I don't believe you love me—not yet. First you have to . . ." This is a false ending, because now we will have to see a scene set in the future to know if the father will meet the terms. Setting terms for the vanquished stalls the ending of the scene. It's just another form of negotiating that ruins scenes.

Enjoy Your Success

When playing the protagonist, it's better to focus your energies on enjoying your success than on making the other characters pay for their past sins. If you're the protagonist, remember that the audience has been rooting for you. If you get what you want and then grind your heel in the face of the other character, we may be sorry we rooted for you and we'll feel cheated. The audience may be saying to themselves, "We thought you were a good guy, but you're just a small, petty jerk." Stay noble. Be big-hearted.

In summary, here are some reasons to conclude the journey definitively: in a well-constructed story, the audience is rooting for a specific outcome. If we answer the question definitively, the audience knows if it got what it wanted (and can react accordingly). We don't always have to answer the question the way the audience wants us to (as long as our choice can be supported by the internal logic of the scene)—we only have to answer it definitively, so the audience can respond.

I saw a terrific example of an unexpected ending in a scene with a confused old woman in a nursing home. She was our protagonist. A very warm and friendly male nurse came into the room to encourage her to get dressed in a nice outfit. They had some verbal exchanges, and he was seemingly intent on helping her get ready for a special visit. The old woman was balking, and confused by what he wanted her to do. As the nurse went to her closet, the old woman followed him and he started to help her into a garment that opened from the back. After her arms were in, he quickly wrapped her in the rest of

When you're the protagonist, it's better to focus your energies on enjoying your success than on making the other characters pay for their past sins. Make the audience glad it rooted for you.

the way (turns out it was a straightjacket, and he was just luring her into it, pretending to be nice). This was a complete surprise to us all, but was fully supported by what we had seen so far. Two improvisers who were watching actually jumped out of their chairs and yelled "NO!" when it happened. They were so upset by the ending that they reenacted the scene later in class, and created a new, happier ending for it.

It's thrilling when an improvised moment can catch the audience so off-guard, and create such a strong response, and of course the only reason we were invested was because the actors had made us care about the old woman and her predicament. This was a case where the protagonist didn't win, and it was still a very satisfying scene.

The other reason to answer the question definitively is so the improviser playing the hero knows if he got what he wanted or not, and can respond accordingly (celebrating success or grieving about failure).

We don't have to give the audience the outcome it was hoping for; we just have to answer the question definitively so the audience can respond.

Fulfill the Promise of the Consequences

The completion of the journey needs to include the consequences laid out earlier in the scene. They should be either manifested or removed. If they're removed, we should know why. In the annual report scene, one of the consequences for not doing what the boss wanted was that the worker would be fired. He wasn't fired in the end because a higher power (the board of directors) prevailed.

Some other ways the consequences may be played out:

- the protagonist feared consequences and those fears were unfounded
- something else (a greater good) is more important than the consequences

I recently saw a lovely example of that last idea. The protagonist was a spoiled princess who was confronted by evil. She thought she had bested the witch, but was tricked into choosing between her own life and saving her kingdom from evil. She chose to drink poison, thereby saving her subjects. It was so great to see an improviser make the selfless choice (with no negotiating!) and accept the consequences as they had been established. The scene was extremely satisfying and touching.

Fulfilling the promise of the consequences is another way of saying *complete the transaction.* As mentioned in chapter 6, this is a simple way to find endings for stories. If you find that you're often in scenes that perk along nicely and then stall when they should end, consider that you may be avoiding completing transactions. When interactions have come to a natural (and complete) resolution, stories feel finished and the audience is satisfied.

Practice Definitive Answers

It's best to practice this step in the course of actual scene work because it tends to be artificial if you use the Round Robin structure, or arbitrarily set up a narrative journey. When practicing the protagonist structure, pay attention to the point in the scene when the audience is ready to know the outcome, when we feel ready to hear the answer to the question. At that point, everyone on stage should strive to answer it as quickly as possible, with no negotiating. The offers may feel fake and goody-goody at first; that's OK. Just keep practicing until finishing scenes crisply feels second nature to you. At that point, you will probably notice that you are able to do it gracefully.

> *Fulfilling the promise of the consequences is another way of saying* COMPLETE THE TRANSACTION.

5. Show How the Protagonist Has Been Changed

All this striving and overcoming of obstacles must result in a new, improved (or at least *changed*) protagonist. Even if the hero failed in his quest, he should be richer for the experience. This step need not take forever to manifest, or be overly clunky or maudlin. Sometimes if we can see the hero in a small moment alone, and if the actor is willing to share the inner life of the character, that's enough. Some stories may call for more information, like a narrator who wraps it up, or tells us what happens in the future. Please use this technique sparingly—more often than not, it's a cop-out. It's much more satisfying if one of the other characters inside the scene can give us the same information.

In addition to knowing how the protagonist has been changed by her journey, we will be interested to know how her relationships have changed, to herself and to others. Self-understanding or a deeper understanding of human nature are logical outcomes of a worthwhile journey.

> *The process of the journey should result in a new, improved (or at least* CHANGED) *protagonist.*

A Variation on the Structure

The examples in this chapter have all been of low-status characters who overcome adversity to achieve their goals. As mentioned earlier, there are other possibilities, such as a high-status protagonist. In order for this to work, the high-status character is usually brought low by circumstance, or may be permanently altered by some life-changing event. Indeed, this is the very definition of tragedy: a flawed central figure is brought low (or killed) by his o'erweening pride, greed, lust for power, etc. King Lear starts out the play as the most powerful person on stage; by the end of the play he has lost everything he holds dear and dies in the knowledge of his folly.

It's tricky to improvise this reversal of the structure, because we take each other at face value when we make and accept offers. If, at the beginning of a scene, someone is throwing his weight around, it is likely that the other improvisers will assume he is trying to endow someone else as the hero. However, if this actor (or his partners) can establish his emotional investment in something important early on, he might succeed in becoming the protagonist.

If your protagonist is a high-status character, the process of the journey is reversed.

The steps in the journey remain the same, but the path the character walks would be reversed. In other words, instead of gathering resources along the way, this protagonist will lose resources. Enemies may increase in number, and friends decrease. The hero becomes less sure of himself the longer he proceeds. By the end of the story, it is the protagonist who acknowledges loss, and the other characters (or Fate/Right/Truth) who are the victors.

At the end of this reversed structure, we still need to see how the hero has been changed by the journey, and this may be the most poignant moment in the story. The once-powerful hero who has lost everything, or whose outlook has been completely altered, will have something to say to the audience that will be worth hearing.

We've looked at how to create a compelling story centering on one person's journey. Now let's look at some additional ideas about improvised stories that will help you pack even more punch into your scenes.

Time

Time behaves differently in stories. The following is a quote from an essay entitled "States of Reading" by Sven Birkerts. The interior quote is from Saul Bellow's book *Humboldt's Gift*:

> Along with this altered sense of time—bound up with it—comes a condensation of reality. Things are linked each to each through association, not physical or chronological proximity. Months, never mind days, are elided in the space of a breath:
>
> "I envied his luck, his talent and his fame, and I went east in May to have a look at him—perhaps to get next to him."
>
> Reality—dull, obstacle-laden reality, which moves all too often at the pace of an intravenous dripper—is reconfigured by the imagination—speeded up, harmonized, made efficient—and served back to us in a far more palatable state, appealing in the extreme.

When reading the excerpt we don't need evidence of every little thing that made Humboldt famous—we take it at face value because we have been told it is so. Improv stories are often hindered by too much unnecessary detail. It probably stems from the fact that we're making it up as we go along, and therefore have no idea where the story is headed, so we lay down tiny stepping stones to help us find our way.

But the audience isn't operating under the same pressure we are. They're making connections and associations (without "physical or chronological proximity") as needed to make sense of the story. This is the reason that after many an improv show an audience member has said to me, "I couldn't get over how tight that story was"—and they were referring to a scene which I thought was a complete narrative mess!

The audience makes connections and associations because they need to. They search for sense and meaning in stories—even poorly sketched ones. So what does this mean for us? It means, for one thing, that we can talk less. Speech is only one way (and often the most tedious way) to convey information. Physical actions, facial expressions, or non-verbal sounds speak

Time behaves differently in stories.

The audience makes connections and associations as necessary to make sense of the story. We don't need to lay down a million tiny stepping-stones for them to find their way.

volumes. All these choices are also quicker than talking. Let's suppose you're in a scene where your boyfriend is making you really angry. You can say you're really angry and get into a long, drawn-out conversation, or you can slap him. I'm not advocating slapping your partners on a regular basis, but in this instance you can see it would be by far the quicker and more powerful choice.

I think we improvisers worry too much. We worry that the audience won't understand an action if they haven't seen every little thing leading up to that action. We're wrong. They will.

A funny thing one sees a lot in improv is a scene where one character says, "I'm not going to stay here and listen to you anymore. I'm leaving." And then they stand there. And stand there. The other improviser can see that they aren't really leaving, so no action is required. Time seems to stand still, and not in a good way.

If the first improviser would just leave (or at least head for the door), the second improviser would have to *move to action* to stop him. Action begets action. Words beget words. Whenever possible, choose an action or an emotion to convey meaning. Not only will it speed up the story, but since actions and emotions are more primal offers, it will probably deepen it as well.

Action begets action. Words beget words.

PACE

To avoid moving stories in a metronomic *plop, plop, plop* of an intravenous dripper, we must know when to speed things up, as well as when to slow them down. This is a skill that takes practice; you can understand it by watching improv scenes, paying close attention to the pace, and noting when things need to go slower, and when faster.

When I talk about pace in scenes, I'm talking about the overall rhythm of the scene, not the timing or delivery of individual lines. Here are some general guidelines about pace.

1. When a really important offer is made, leave some space (silence) around it. Suppose you've reached the point in a scene about unrequited love where the hero finally gets the courage to say "I love you" to the object of his affection. This is an important moment, and the other actor shouldn't rush to

answer right away. Let the moment shimmer in the air for a second—give yourself and your partner a chance to be affected by the moment. Give the *audience* a chance.

2. In a comic scene, apply the same idea. Let's say you're in a bungling burglar scene and just as you approach the safe in the vault, you announce that you forgot your safe-cracking tools. This deserves a beat of silence or two. If your partner jumps on it too quickly, the importance of the offer will be missed (and the comedy may be lost).

3. If you're in a confrontation scene, and the pace is starting to pick up—let it! An out-of-control feeling is great for scenes like these. If you're feeling nervous, the audience probably is too. Strive to be out-of-control, off-balance; those are the moments when truly exciting things can happen.

4. If the protagonist is at a turning point in the story, slow down and explore it fully.

5. Once a decision has been made by one of the characters (which often means the story slowed down momentarily), move to the action *quickly*.

6. Don't work up to things—just do them.

7. When you're near the end of the story, let the momentum increase. The audience often sees the end of the story long before we do, and at that point they simply want the satisfaction of seeing it played out. Imagine yourself as a horse-for-hire. If you've ever been horseback riding on rented horses (as I did when I was a kid in Arizona), you may have experienced this: on the first half of the ride, the horse plods along at an unimaginably slow pace, as though you're leading it to the glue factory instead of out onto open land for a nice run. Once you reach the halfway point, your poky old horse suddenly turns into greased lightning and heads at a full gallop back to the stable. It's like he can smell the stable, and can't wait to get the saddle off and his nose buried in a feed bag.

Don't work up to things. Just do them.

Smell the stable.

When I'm directing an improv scene, and we in the audience can sense the end of the scene, I often yell, "Smell the stable!" This usually works nicely, unless the improvisers haven't heard the anecdote. In that case, things just get downright weird ...

Realism

We get 'way too worked up about realism. It's overrated. Especially when it comes to theater—*especially* when it comes to improv. We're not bound by the constraints of time or place—so why should we be bound by realistic behavior? At a minimum, theater should explore heightened reality, and at its most extreme, out-and-out fantasy. That's the power of theater: to transport the audience beyond their everyday experience.

I'm surprised how many improv scenes take place in the here-and-now, with very ordinary characters. While there's nothing wrong with that, I don't know why the *majority* of scenes are set that way. We have so many wonderful places to go, both real and imaginary—why should we limit ourselves to the workplace and the kitchen? How many times have you seen this: a scene is set in an exotic locale, and everyone acts as though they're back in America, in the office or the kitchen? In other words, the actors don't immerse themselves in the setting; they're just paying lip service to it. In these situations, it's not uncommon for the improvisers to resort to gags in order to set themselves apart from the locale. This is a way of winking at the audience and saying, "I know this scene isn't very good, set as it is in Timbuktu—so I'll stand here and make pop-cultural references instead of investing myself in the scene."

A much better use of that improviser's energy would be to throw herself into the scene with abandon and see what happens—to create, with her partners, her version of Timbuktu, instead of reducing everything back to a copy of everyday life.

Let the hero in your journey take you by the hand. Be willing to invest in the quest, to explore along with the audience the unseen terrain of human experience. Go to places you didn't know existed until three minutes ago. Don't be satisfied to act out your same old life, over and over again; improv is standing in the shadows, beckoning us to live new lives.

Playing with Fire
Creating Richer Characters

Most of us feel lucky if we can grab a funny voice before we run on stage. A kooky walk is gravy. Everything happens so fast in an improv scene that sometimes it seems like a miracle if we're facing the right direction and not walking through walls. The idea of playing full characters can seem like a pipe dream.

The challenges before us are these: how can we play distinct characters who are different from us (and from each other)? How can we bring emotional truthfulness to lives we haven't experienced? How can we follow our instincts on stage, but manifest them through other bodies, voices, and emotional realities?

It *is* possible. It begins with trusting something you can't see. Call it the collective unconscious, or genetic memory, or reincarnation. Name it the artistic process, the magic If, or the relinquishment of the self. It doesn't matter what you call it; there's a force at work in the theater. We are conduits, and that force, that energy, passes through us to the audience.

Strong characters are born when we surrender to the force, not when we try to bend it to our will. So it's a matter of preparation (practice) and then letting go. Full, rich characters are waiting for us like ghosts in the wings. And those spirits

> *There's a force at work in the theater. We are the conduits and that force, that energy, passes through us to the audience.*

Full, rich characters are waiting for us like ghosts in the wings. And those spirits find their way into us through as many doors as we are willing to leave open.

find their way into us through as many doors as we are willing to leave open. One way to open those doors is to stretch our capabilities by experimenting with different points of origin for characters: physical, vocal, and emotional.

All these points of origin can be explored in practice. Physical and vocal practice tunes your instrument and is critically important for well-rounded play. But it's the *emotional* practice that will bring your characters into full relief.

The more you practice, the more flexible you will be, and the greater will be your acting vocabulary. Increased fluidity and an open mind will coax the ghosts out of the wings and onto your stage. Improvisers rarely have the luxury of costumes to suggest character, so your body, voice and emotional life are your greatest assets.

Physical Origins

Starting a character from the physical plane is a form of "outside/in" acting. This means that changes you make in your walk, posture, weight distribution, agility, etc., will inform and affect your internal state. If I'm playing an old woman with arthritis in her hips and hands, that will affect my ability to respond quickly and it may also affect my mood. Our bodies will respond truthfully to given circumstances if we keep our brains out of the way. In other words, if I can move as though my body hurts, it will change the way I walk, sit, talk, and even breathe; it may also change the way I feel inside. If I stay connected to my body and pay attention to the impulses I feel and *follow them*, I should be able to create and maintain a believable character. This will only happen if I do the practice long enough to let changes occur. The more I practice, the more able I become to follow my body and let myself be transformed by it.

How do you practice physical characterization? Here are some simple acting exercises you can do by yourself or in class.

Moving Centers Exercise

This is a solo exercise, but all the players work at the same time. It helps if you have a large, empty room to work in. Imagine that your character's essence is concentrated in her forehead. She leads from that center.

Now begin moving around the room and pay attention to any other changes taking place. Do you distribute your weight differently? Is your stride changed at all? Let your whole body be affected by the center. You may move your arms differently; your legs and feet may be operating in a new way. What are you feeling or thinking? Is your character highly intelligent, or on the stupid side? A character may feel proud and connected to their essential "center," or be very repressed and embarrassed about it.

Return to your normal walk and shake out your arms, legs and head. Walk neutrally for a moment, then create a *different* character who leads from the forehead. Now repeat the exercise, placing the character's center in different places: the heart, stomach, groin, knees, ankles, etc. Between each character you create, return to your normal walk. You can lead from your left shoulder, or your right foot. Just be sure to move around long enough in each stage to let changes overtake you. Notice any emotional effects.

Let's look at some of the centers in more detail. Leading from the heart center can produce very strong emotional reactions in improvisers. A person who moves as though attached by a cord to the sky (lifting the breastbone up and out) often looks very happy, spiritual and loving. A character whose heart center is caved in may feel lonely, damaged, or sad.

Working from the stomach center is fun. Walk with your stomach stuck way out in front of you. Now let your body rebalance itself around the protruding stomach. You may feel expanded, slow, superior or bloated. Conversely, walking with the stomach center tucked in can create a feeling of insecurity, want, or fear. Changing the way we balance our weight over our stomachs usually affects everything about the way we move.

The groin center is the power triangle. A character that leads brazenly from the groin will appear very sexually confident (or at least sexually *active*), while a character that hides and protects the groin area will seem sexually repressed or fearful.

Knees are worth fiddling with because many age adjustments can be made with a slight alteration of the knees. Imagine a toddler you know who has just learned to walk unassisted. Picture how their feet bang against the floor, and how high they raise their knees. Toddlers don't yet know quite how long their legs are, or how far away the floor. Old age can be similarly explored via the knees. Arthritis often strikes the joints, and even an older person without arthritis will move slowly when sitting and standing, usually experiencing a stiffness of the joints. By simply moving the knee joint more slowly you will automatically appear older.

Feet are another wonderful (sometimes overlooked) center to start from. Imagine a ballet dancer who prances and leaps through life. Now try a dock worker with a foot injury, slowly dragging his leg and gingerly placing the damaged foot with each step he takes.

Animals and People

Most actors have had to imitate an animal at some point in their theatrical training, and although it may seem silly, it can help you move differently in your body. Here's a variation on the old standard that I've found useful: Try playing around with being a panther, and make specific choices about your circumstances. What time of day is it? Are you hungry? How old are you? Male or female? Pregnant? Prowling for food? Being hunted? After you have acted on these questions as fully as possible, return to neutral, and then play *another* panther with completely different circumstances. If you were old the first time, be a cub this time. If you were hungry the first time, this time you have just eaten. You get the picture. Repeat the exercise using other animals: snakes, puppies, squirrels, birds, etc. Practice two of each animal.

In addition to animals, try kids, old people, foreigners, and people in other time periods. Do you hold a stereotypical view of New York cab drivers? Then see how many *different* New York cab drivers you can find in yourself. Not all of them hate their jobs. Not all of them are from other countries. Not all of them are men.

Be Renaissance painters, cavemen, Spanish Inquisitors, explorers, pirates, and cable repair people. Try playing the opposite sex—and do it for real. See how far into the psyche of the opposite sex you can delve.

How many different versions of a character type can you discover?

Again, be sure to expand your viewpoint. Not everyone responds to things the way you do. If you have played a woman with arthritis, try playing six other women with arthritis, all of whom react to the condition differently.

To stretch your range of characters beyond the limits of your own imagination, have your partners create new characters for you (see Character Swap on page 34).

Vocal Origins

Some improvisers can create entire characters just by changing their voices. Vocal work includes dialects and accents, changing the pitch of your voice, the clarity of your tone, the rate at which you speak, and the placement of your pauses. If you can, take a vocal class to learn some of the technical aspects of vocal acting. Even if you can't take formal training, it's easy and fun to play around with vocal changes on your own.

Dialects, Accents and Gibberish

In improv, when we talk about dialects, we are usually referring to foreign accents. The exception to this would be dialects of America or other English-speaking countries. In those instances, the improviser would not only pronounce words differently, but would use regional grammar and vocabulary to distinguish the dialect. For example, Cockney is a dialect of British English and encompasses slang phrases as well as specific word pronunciations.

The best way to get adept at dialects is to listen to and practice them. You can buy dialect tapes at drama bookstores, and you can record movies on television and then try to mimic what you hear. Listen for the major substitutions that are the essence of the dialect. For example, one of the major substitutions for high-class American Southern is dropping the final "r" sound (thus, "river" becomes "rivuh" and "murderer" becomes "murderuh"). Don't worry about being perfect; at first it's more important to make the main substitutions than it is to hit them all. And it's important that you can speak at a normal rate (unless speed is one of the other markers of the dialect). As with the physical work, try not to pigeonhole yourself with stereotypical notions about dialects. I have known some

Expand your viewpoint. Not everyone responds to things the way you do.

Voice work is one of the few improv skills you can practice by yourself, so do your homework.

extremely fast-talking Southerners, and some slow-speaking New Yorkers. Yes, really.

Practice the basic vowel and consonant substitutions and go from there. Remember that many factors about your character will affect the way he is speaking, particularly his emotional state and other circumstances of the scene.

Try reading the newspaper or a novel out loud in a foreign accent. The more you do this, the more comfortable you will be trying an accent out on stage. Pay attention to any status or emotional changes that you feel when speaking with a foreign accent. While Brits are often swooned over for their elegant accents, people from other countries are often made to feel inferior for speaking English with an accent. If you've ever traveled to France and spoken French with an American accent, you know exactly what I'm talking about.

Gibberish is made-up language, either intended to mimic a real language such as Italian, or a completely fabricated language like Martian. If you get endowed in a scene as being from Mars, you will want to be able to speak your native tongue with ease.

When practicing gibberish, pay attention to making it sound like a real language. The sound of a language, the vowels and consonants, are only a part of the whole. Musicality, vocal placement, and emphasis on vowels vs. consonants convey a great deal of meaning. Use inflection to convey sentence structure. Repeating words your partner has used will convey the impression of an actual language. Think about Italian and German for a moment. The musicality of each language is very different, and you would never mistake one for the other. It's the same with gibberish. You can convey a lot about the "culture" of your fictitious country by the way you speak its language.

Pitch

Try this experiment. Read the previous paragraph aloud in your normal voice. Now read it again while placing your pitch much higher. Try it again, this time making your voice much lower than usual. Each time you change your pitch, let yourself be changed in other ways. Does a higher pitch make you feel younger or less significant? How about a lower pitch? Does it make you feel more authoritative? Simply changing your pitch can conjure up a lot of other differences in the characters you play. What if your character is applying for a job, and has a high, squeaky voice? Is he going to be as confident as the candidate sitting next to him with a low, newscaster-type voice?

A note to female improvisers: when we get emotional in scenes, our voices often start to rise in pitch. Pretty soon only dogs can hear us. We must be vigilant and remember to use our resonant chest voices when something exciting is happening. I call it the "Medea voice." It starts deep within the center of the earth, travels up through our legs, gathers force in our guts, emotion in our hearts, and comes blasting out our mouths. It's not a pinched, whiny voice—it's the voice of Greek tragedy. It can be heard in the back row. By humans.

Use caution when you change your pitch. Find a range that you can sustain comfortably. Always warm up your voice before improvising, especially if you will be doing a lot of vocal character work. Make sure you are breathing fully, and letting lots of air "lubricate" your vocal chords. Avoid squeezing off your sound to raise your pitch, and pay attention to the fatigue factor that sets in when practicing. Never choose a growly or raspy voice in a scene that will be impossible to maintain. Vocal cord damage is no fun.

Women: when we get emotional in scenes, our voices often get so high only dogs can hear us. Practice your "Medea voice." It starts in the center of the earth and comes bursting out of you like a volcano.

Rate

Do you know someone who never takes a breath when they're on a talking streak? Of course, they must be breathing, but they've mastered the art of the sneak breath, which doesn't take up much time, or allow anyone else to enter the conversation. Do you know someone else who always pauses before speaking? Do you know someone who speaks so slowly that you think you'll celebrate your next birthday before they finish? Do you find yourself making assumptions or judgments about these people based on their rate of speech? The rate at which you speak identifies you. This involves not only the speed, but also the placement and number of pauses you use.

A person who stammers seems uncertain, even if they're not. A chatterbox usually strikes us as the nervous or narcissistic type. People who speak slowly and thoughtfully often come across as intelligent.

Take these assumptions into account as you practice changing your rate of speech. If you're in a scene that needs a dignified college professor, try speaking slowly and distinctly, as though you are used to everyone in the room hanging on your every word. Likewise, if you're in a scene about the Mob, and you are being interrogated by Mr. Big, you might want to try chattering away to see if it affects your character emotionally.

Tone

Vocal tone changes depending on where the tone is placed in the "mask." You may have heard singers talking about the mask, which is the front part of the face including the nasal passages, nose and cheekbone area. A singer with a bright, clear voice usually places her tone in the mask, where resonation is loud and vibrant. Conversely, a spoken or sung tone placed in the back of the throat sounds swallowed and doesn't carry as far.

One of the most basic responsibilities of the improviser is to be heard clearly both by her fellow players and the audience. After achieving that, there is room for experimentation with vocal placement.

Some changes to try:

- put your voice up into your nose, and produce the most nasal sound possible
- open the back of your throat and push a lot of air through as you speak
- if you ordinarily speak in your head voice (the higher register), try speaking so that your tone resonates in your chest for a deeper, richer sound

Pause Placement

Pause placement can change the effect of your speech even if you're not altering it in any other way. Experiment with different pause placement. Try putting a pause near the very end of your sentence, right before you conclude. This makes your partners (and the audience) wait for what you've got to say (as you can imagine, this is a double-edged sword!). Or, pause before you begin speaking, which will make whatever you say next seem well thought out. (For a detailed discussion of how pause placement can affect status, read Keith Johnstone's *Impro*.)

As with the physical work, vocal practice stretches your instrument. Speaking in a new way can trigger different emotional reactions and coax out characters you didn't know you had dwelling within you.

Emotional Origins for Characters

Now comes the hard part. As difficult as it is to shake ourselves out of our physical and vocal habits, it's nothing compared to the challenge of finding emotional perspectives different from our own. Like all the other techniques in this section, your emotional work will expand with practice, but this is an area where you may find it riskier to take chances.

One of the biggest gaps I see in most improv is that players don't experiment much with emotionality. Even players who have a good command of their physical and vocal instruments don't tend to stray too far from their own emotional underpinnings. And that's no wonder. It's scary as hell to even *improvise*, let alone leave behind the tools we use to cope with uncertainty, such as our natural pessimism, or cheerfulness, or whatever arrows you happen to stock in your quiver.

But here's the deal: the more willing we are to try on other peoples' lives, the greater the chance that we will be expanded in the process. If we limit our responses in scenes to our own little set of neuroses and habits, not only will our scenes be tediously similar, but we'll also miss the opportunity to experience the world in a new way.

The opportunity for new experience is the great lure of improv. I submit that it's the main reason that improv is so exhilarating when we first try it. So why do we stop the experiment once we've achieved a certain level of improv skill? I think it's because we know that it won't just be our improv ideas that will be challenged; it will be our whole way of going about our lives. We may be forced to examine our patterns, habits and responses to life, and we're very attached to them.

Is that so terrible?

Whether it is or not, we have to be braver than we thought we were, and willing, at least for the time we're onstage, to be *different people*. We have to see that there's more than one way

The more willing we are to try on other peoples' lives, the greater the chance that we will be expanded in the process.

Improvising challenges us to look at the patterns in our lives. Our hair-trigger reactions to situations are just habit. They aren't necessarily the best choice in a given set of circumstances, they're just what we've grown comfortable with.

to skin an emotional cat. Our hair-trigger reactions to situations are just habit; they aren't necessarily the best choice in a given set of circumstances; they're just what we've grown comfortable with.

For example, I have this odd thing I do that I'm working hard to change. Whenever a friend, student, or colleague says, "Carol, could I talk to you about something?" my immediate thought is that I've done something wrong, and they're angry with me. Nine times out of ten, the person has some personal difficulty they want help with. The tenth time it may be a compliment they want to give me in private. Now, without going into any detail about why I respond this way, the point is that I do. And that means that the characters I play tend to respond to the same stimuli in the same way. Ugh! That's so limiting!

The solution? To practice playing people with different emotional bases from mine. To play women who always expect the best, who always win, who don't care what anyone else thinks of them; mean women, bitter women, carefree women, clowns, executives, window-washers—whoever I need to play to allow myself to experience other emotional realities. The more I practice, the easier it becomes to let myself be overtaken by other lives—and surprised by the outcomes of interactions.

To stretch your emotional range, try playing characters with these emotional qualities:

- extremely needy
- self-sufficient
- optimistic
- spiteful
- joyous
- pessimistic
- ebullient
- expectant
- naive
- sorrowful

Remember, experiment with these not only as emotional starting points, but also as the belief systems in which these characters operate. For example, a pessimistic person almost always expects the worst, whether it involves a date, a job promotion, or leaving the house on a cloudy day. That pessimism affects every choice the person makes, and it hinders his ability to change. The same holds for any emotional "truth" a character is fixed on. That doesn't mean that a pessimist never smiles, but he may be extremely surprised when some small thing goes well. Don't use these belief systems as an excuse not to change; rather, they are a way to play characters with some consistency.

You may have to really push yourself to do this kind of work, because trying on other emotional lives means you may come up against your *own* belief systems and be challenged to look at them differently. You may find that the emotional ruts you are in aren't serving you anymore.

Showing Different Sides of Characters

It's our responsibility to show the audience as many aspects of our characters as possible. Even in a one-minute monologue, we should see at least two facets of the character, her thoughts, values, emotional life, etc. For instance, if I'm doing a monologue and playing a high-status, confident businesswoman, at some point in that monologue I should experience a shift so that I can portray that same woman when she is feeling insecure, or lonely, or regretful about some aspect of her life. Or, the second aspect could be a girlish crush she has on a co-worker. Anything that will show another side of her. I want to avoid getting stuck in a rut right off the bat.

Just because a character operates in a certain belief system is no reason he can't have different aspects to his emotional makeup. Even our pessimist in the example above will have other sides to his personality. Maybe he was very hopeful as a child, and still lets that part of himself out once in awhile. Or maybe, instead of being a defeated pessimist, he's sometimes angry and sadistic toward others.

And don't forget that in the best scenes, characters are *changed*. Very often, we improvisers will refuse to change, saying, "But my character wouldn't do that!" We share this misconception with our colleagues in scripted theater. Well, guess what? Your character is capable of doing anything—which is the premise of theater. And the most interesting theater is predicated on the promise

Don't use a character's belief system as an excuse not to change; look at these beliefs as a way to play characters with some consistency.

It's our responsibility to show the audience as many different aspects of our characters as possible.

Theater promises that people will behave OUT *of character.*

that the audience will see people behaving *out* of character. That's how you get a play like *Agnes of God*, where a young, devoted nun kills her own baby. Nobody would pay money to see a two-hour exploration of a day in the life of a real nun: prayers, work, meals, prayers, bedtime.

Use the following exercises to practice creating multi-faceted characters.

Three Stages of Life—Monologue

In this exercise, an improviser will do three monologues, each lasting one minute. The player will portray the same character throughout. In the first monologue, the actor will show us one side of the character. In the second monologue, some amount of time has passed (either backward or forward in time), and we see another aspect of the same character. In the third round, we see yet another stage in this character's life, and we see how his experiences and choices have affected him emotionally. An example:

Monologue 1: A tough street punk tells about his exploits robbing a liquor store with some friends.

Monologue 2: The same man, a few years later, in prison. He is still tough, but older now and more bitter, less cocky and optimistic about his life. He tells us his girlfriend had a baby just before he got arrested the last time.

Monologue 3: The same man, several years later, sitting in a run-down apartment. He is talking about his son, now twenty, who is getting into trouble. The man is angry with his son, and talks about "kids who don't know no better." He seems not to be taking any responsibility for his part in his son's choices, but underneath we see that he is sorry and regretful.

This was a cycle of scenes I saw in class. It was very moving because the improviser was willing to explore several sides of the character. It's important when you start working with this exercise to keep the first monologue fairly simple. This is not a narrative exercise. The purpose is to explore character, and it's good to remember that the most telling moments often take place between the lines (remember the Hot Object exercise? See page 40). When a character is pausing, groping for words, we have the chance to see into the character. I remember one improviser who hardly spoke at all during the first monologue—she was showing us the character rather than talking about her. In her manner, the way she sat in the chair and looked nervously around, dropping her eyes and folding her hands in her lap—we got a very clear picture before the character ever opened her mouth. In the subsequent monologues, when the character spoke more confidently, we saw the change for ourselves. This is the difference between *showing* us the character and *telling* us the character.

I mentioned earlier that the monologues may move backward and forward in time. When the actor chooses to go back in time, we can see what influences created the character we saw in a previous monologue. If we have just seen an adult who is a mean, nasty, aggressive jerk, it might be interesting for us to see a monologue from his childhood where we see what caused him to become that adult.

The amount of time that passes between the stages can be minimal. It's possible to show different aspects of the character which are brought out by changes in the character's situation. For example, if in Scene A we see a student who is studying for his SAT's, the next monologue might be about taking the SAT's, and the last one about getting his scores in the mail. As long as the actor shows us several different aspects of the character, it doesn't matter how much or how little time has elapsed.

When first working with the exercise, I usually limit each monologue to one minute. This encourages the improvisers to be brief and to talk less. It's also good practice to get to the heart of the matter as quickly as possible. When done in performance, each monologue can be a bit longer.

Once you've had a chance to explore characters with the solo exercise, try the same structure with two-person scenes, as described below.

Remember, the most telling moments often take place between the lines. Trust silence.

Three Stages of Life—Scenes

This is the same basic exercise, except that two improvisers do a short scene. Two more short scenes follow the first. The improvisers are revealing not only

> their characters at different stages of their lives, but also a *relationship* at different points in time. It's great to practice different aspects of relationship, to remind ourselves that even in a single short scene, we should see more than one side of the relationship.

These two exercises are also useful if you are working on long-form improvisation. Long forms often suffer from characters that remain exactly the same every time they come onstage. These exercises will help you play recurring characters with more breadth and depth.

Putting It All Together

The Character Swap exercise and Character Interactions (detailed in chapter 3) provide wonderful opportunities to create full-blown characters very different from ourselves. If you're lucky enough to be playing in an established ensemble, you can challenge your partners to expand their character ranges by creating the types of characters you never see them play. For example, I was recently working with an improviser who tends to play likable, low-status characters. I created a pompous, know-it-all, stiff-bodied man for him, and he unleashed a side of himself none of us had ever seen. Wonderful, edgy narrative flowed out of him unbidden, and he used his body in a completely new way. And it required very little effort on his part. Because the character was created by someone else and given to him, all he had to do was run with it. He was absolved of any *responsibility* for the character, and enjoyed the freedom that entailed.

In knitting together the aspects of character (body, voice, and emotion), leave room for the fourth entity, the ghosts in the wings. Remember that the body and voice can only inhabit the present moment; when you free them fully, a flood of life, emotion, and experience can come rushing through you and onto the stage.

Choosing a Character to Serve the Scene

Once you've become flexible and fluent in several different types of characters, the question still remains: How do you choose the character that will best serve the scene? Watch carefully, pay attention to your instincts, and then jump in and do your best.

What are some of the reasons a scene needs an additional character? Sometimes the scene is failing narratively; sometimes the improvisers are all mirroring each other's tone, rhythm, or emotional state; sometimes a new character has been called for, and you just need to go in and fulfill that call.

When you're practicing improv, or watching shows, start looking at scenes with an eye toward what kind of character the scene most needs. Let's look at some specific examples.

When Everyone Is Mirroring

Mirroring happens all the time in improv, and I've noticed it tends to happen a great deal when we are doing genre work. An example of this came up for me a few years back. My partners were doing a Tennessee Williams scene, and they had established a good beginning for the scene: relationships and names were established, and the weather was (of course) hot. Then the scene began to falter. I stood in the wings and had a sudden flash that the main problem was one of mirroring. Everyone was speaking in a very slow Southern drawl, and they all looked as if they might keel over at any moment from heat prostration. So I chose to come in full of life, energy and sexuality, speaking in a tumble of words, and blasting into the room physically, in order to shake things up a bit.

The instinct was a good one, and that one small moment of jolting energy helped get the scene back in motion. It also energized the other improvisers. My role in the overall scene was fairly small, but the contribution at the moment I made it was extremely useful.

Improvisers love to stand in clumps on stage, and we love to mirror each other. We do both for the same reason: as long as we don't differentiate ourselves on stage, as long as we're all doing the same thing, then we can't be singled out as being wrong. Unfortunately, this leads to some very homogenous scene work. When watching a scene that has been afflicted with mirroring, make a conscious choice of a very different tone, rhythm, emotional, vocal or physical state, and enter the scene, bringing as much fresh energy as you can muster. If you can also add a really helpful narrative offer, so much the better.

Improvisers love to mirror each other. As long as we don't differentiate ourselves on stage, then we can't be singled out for being wrong.

When a Character Has Been Specifically Described

If two characters are talking about "mean ol' Mr. Harkness," you probably know that you need to come into the scene and be mean and old. Most improvisers will fulfill this endowment without too much trouble. But the trouble often comes a moment or two later, when Mr. Harkness has "been mean" and is now standing around, unsure of what to do next.

Pay attention to the purpose you need to serve in the scene. Have you been endowed as a villain, a friend, or an onlooker? Let your character choices grow out of your purpose in the scene. Remember that you were called in relative to some action that was going on at the time. In other words, if two boys were throwing rocks at Mr. Harkness's windows, you will come on as their worst nightmare. If, on the other hand, the scene was about one old woman chatting to another at a church social and pointing at mean ol' Mr. Harkness, his role would be quite different. It would be lovely to see a crabby old man trying to ask a woman to dance.

And hey—when you sense you've fulfilled your purpose in the scene, *get off the stage*.

When the Scene Needs a Specific Human Quality

Sometimes a scene needs a character to illustrate some quality, such as goodness, but nobody in the scene is doing it. Let's say you're in a scene set during the Salem Witch trials, which includes a persecuted heroine, the prosecutors, and townspeople (who are yelling for blood). The scene may need the voice of an innocent (like in "The Emperor's New Clothes") to turn the story around. You could be the innocent. Be as pure and loving as you possibly can. See if you can turn the hardened hearts of the prosecutors into butter.

The reverse may be needed in a scene as well. Maybe the scene needs cold-hearted villainy, and nobody on stage is up to the task. Make yourself as cold, ruthless, and uncaring as you possibly can, then go in and have a field day. Torture the protagonist. Belittle the secondary characters as spineless wimps. Scorch the earth with your badness. Go, baby! Half the fun of improvising is that we get to manifest all the sides of ourselves that we would never, ever in a million years show in public. I had a blast once in an improvised musical when I played a spiteful old woman who hated orphans. I sang a song called

"What Good Are Orphans?" where I extolled their uses as cobblestones, as furniture, and for kicking for pleasure. It was delicious to be so morally incorrect, so hateful, and so mean. (And between you and me, I think I worked out some stuff from earlier in the week.)

When the Action Needs to Move Along

Sometimes scenes are doing fine, but they get stuck and need a nudge to get going again. Café scenes often suffer from this malaise, as do most scenes in the dressing room of a performer. The time-honored appearance of the waiter or the stage manager is often the best choice in these circumstances. But what *kind* of waiter is needed? Neutral, or with a specific personality? Should you enter and leave again quickly, or stay on stage as an auxiliary character?

Your best bet is to follow your instincts and give something a shot. Do your best to serve the scene, and remember to pursue your own pleasure as well. Come out as the waiter and refuse to leave. Become extremely emotional. Make yourself pivotal to the scene. It's fun to bust all the rules once in awhile.

We have a symbiotic relationship with the characters we play. Without us, they remain ghosts in the wings, detached spirits of possibility. Without them, we stay shackled to the limitations of our own experience. Together we create unique visions of reality; we can transform *what always was* into *what might be*.

Notes

Acting Like a Human
Objectives and Tactics

Have you ever noticed how often improv characters seem to be doing something for no reason? You'll be watching a scene about a student/teacher conference, and suddenly the actor playing the student will start singing, or raging, or crying, and you don't have the vaguest idea why.

Or how about this? A scene has started, and the improvisers are wandering around, listlessly making offers that don't go anywhere. Instead of the usual crazed energy, the scene has no energy at all. The players look lost and unhappy. This is often the point where someone tries to energize the scene by shouting and waving his arms.

In real life people don't careen around rooms like pinballs. Neither do we float purposeless and inert through our days. We all have reasons for the things we do, even if those reasons don't make sense to anyone else. Our characters should have reasons, too. While unmotivated action is false, lack of action is also false. Both destroy authenticity on stage and usually the story goes out the window, too.

But there's this totally cool thing that can turn you into a powerhouse of meaning and motivation. It's called *playing your objective*.

In chapter 2 we looked briefly at objectives and how they can simplify scene work. Objectives play a much larger part in good improvising, because the pursuit of objectives gives a throughline to a character's behavior, connects us to our partners, and creates endless opportunities for change. (In the example above, singing, raging or crying might all be acceptable actions if we understood *what the character was hoping for as a result*.)

Every person in a scene wants something (their objective), and takes action to achieve it (tactics). The tactics a character uses to get what she wants may be physical, verbal, or emotional. She will use one tactic until it becomes clear that it's unsuccessful, and then she'll change tactics and try something else.

Objectives and tactics have been part of scripted acting for years; now we'll borrow the concept to make our improv more authentic (and easier). In scripted theater, the actor decides after studying the text what his objectives and actions will be. When we improvise, we don't decide on objectives *ahead* of time; rather we'll let them emerge out of the first moments of the scene. To understand how objectives work, try the following exercises.

Objectives give us a throughline to a character's behavior, connect us to our partners, and create endless opportunities for change.

Solo Objectives

This is a solo exercise, performed in front of your fellow improvisers. Use the objectives listed in Appendix B. Each improviser will be assigned an objective and will attempt to accomplish it. Here are some guidelines for the exercise: Take action to achieve your objective—don't "logic it out" ahead of time—physically take action. Really believe you will accomplish your goal. Keep trying new tactics until you accomplish it or we tell you to stop.

After everyone has done the exercise, talk together about what you noticed. Here are the most common observations I've heard:

- "It was fascinating to watch people pursuing their objectives, even if it was obvious they wouldn't succeed."
- "It was *more* satisfying if we knew they wouldn't succeed."

- "When the actor switched tactics I was completely drawn in."
- "I started to believe she would succeed."
- "The people who really believed they would succeed were the most interesting to watch."
- "I was surprised several times by the tactics people chose."
- "When I was up there, I was completely unself-conscious!"

You'll note when you look at the list of objectives that some of them are easy to achieve, others more difficult. For instance, the objective "to eat something" will only require the actor to find some food and eat it (this shouldn't be too difficult in a room full of performers). The objective "using only your body, touch opposite walls of this room at the same time" is a bit trickier (and one of my personal favorites).

If you receive one of the easy objectives, such as "eat something"—do it as directly as possible. Look for food; when you find it, eat it. Avoid the urge to *pretend* to look for food. This exercise isn't about pretending or performing, it's about doing—for real. You'll notice that the instant an actor is pretending to do something, we lose interest in watching him.

When pursuing an objective, the more concrete, the better. The objective "feel better about yourself" is not only difficult to do, but the audience has no way of knowing if you have succeeded or not, since we can't see inside you.

Remember, we're incorporating objectives not only for our benefit, but to increase the audience's enjoyment of our work. While it isn't essential that they know exactly what we're pursuing (although that's ideal), they do need to see that we have a goal we're working toward.

In scene work, objectives are most useful if they are phrased in the following manner: "I want _____ from him." There is a school of thought that objectives can be more open-ended, such as "to dominate." I prefer the former model for two reasons: 1) I must stay connected at all times to my partner to see if he is going to give me what I want (as opposed to merely "acting dominant," which could be done in a vacuum), and 2) there will be some concrete way I will know if I have succeeded. For

Go after your objective in the most direct way possible.

example, if I've chosen, "I want forgiveness from him," I'll know I have succeeded if he forgives me. If instead, I chose, "I want to stop feeling guilty," that has less to do with my partner than it does with me. (Ah—just like life!)

One of the lovely things about this solo exercise is that it reminds us how fascinating physical action can be. Very few of the suggested objectives require speaking, yet they all produce interesting moments.

What I've noticed when we start using objectives in scene work is that an actor will often say, "Well, it's obvious I'm not going to get my objective—he's never going to fall in love with me!" And nine times out of ten, the actor was playing the scene as if failure was a foregone conclusion. Pursuing an objective half-heartedly is almost worse than not pursuing one at all. If you don't believe you will succeed, you'll be no fun to watch.

Just as in the solo exercise, you have to believe you will succeed at every moment you're in the scene. After trying one tactic *with all your heart*, if you haven't succeeded, try another tactic *with all your heart*. Which brings us to another important idea: pick an objective that's going to be fun to pursue. Then the likelihood goes up that you'll remain connected to your partner and interested in your success.

The following exercises will help you experiment with objectives in two-person scenes. After each exercise, discuss how the objectives affected the quality of the interaction between players.

Pursuing an objective half-heartedly is almost worse than not pursuing one at all. If you don't believe you will succeed, you'll be no fun to watch.

Two-Person Silent Objectives

Each player secretly decides on a physical objective involving her partner. For instance, my objective may be to touch my partner's knee. Her objective may be to always stand in front of me. We will begin a silent interaction, each trying different tactics to achieve our goals. It's important that we respond to each other at all times (remember Torso Fighting on page 68?). In other words, we're not only pursuing our own objectives; we're reacting to our partner's tactics as well. We continue until one or both of us have succeeded in getting our objective.

Do the exercise once more. This time each improviser is trying to get the *other* person to do something physical, e.g., "I want my partner to hug me." Note how this changes the quality of the interaction, and also the tactics employed.

In the next exercise the players will pursue objectives while speaking pre-assigned lines.

Two-Person Scenes with Script

In this exercise, each actor will have only one line of dialogue that they will repeat again and again. The lines are assigned in advance. You can use the lines in Appendix B or make up your own. Before receiving their dialogue, each improviser secretly chooses an objective in the scene. For instance, one player might choose "to borrow money from her" and the other improviser, "to get him to respect me." Then they receive their lines, for example, "Would you like fries with that?" and "You're an awful waiter." The actors then improvise a scene, speaking only their scripted lines and using their bodies, faces, and emotional inner lives to try different tactics.

This exercise illustrates the point that the words we speak are not as important as all the other ways in which we communicate with each other. Tone of voice, physicality, emotion—all these are called into play when we are trying to get something from another person. And because the improvisers are freed up from having to create dialogue, they can focus instead on the interaction.

When playing the scene, stay open to both sending and *receiving* information. The offers you get from your partner will stimulate you to switch tactics.

Scenes with Assigned Objectives

This is the opposite of the previous exercise. Both players receive objectives to play, and start a scene, improvising all their dialogue. The interaction should unfold naturally, each player adjusting to the offers of the other. This gives players a chance to practice improvised

> scenes with objectives without having to think up the objective on the spot.
> See Appendix B for suggestions.

Now the improvisers are ready to play open scenes (with no suggestions) in which the objectives emerge out of the interaction. Let's look at how that works.

THE FIRST INTERACTION

The first moments of a scene are very important, because it is in those moments that we make contact with our partners, sending and receiving all sorts of subtle messages. We use physical positions, facial expressions, and emotional noises to set the stage for the interaction to come. Each of us can also use those first moments to let the objectives emerge that we will follow throughout the scene.

Let's say I'm on stage alone, washing dishes and looking worried. My partner enters, perhaps with an angry look and attitude. In that moment I can follow my instincts and surmise that I've done something wrong. I can then choose an objective for myself, such as getting his forgiveness. My next offers will be the actions I take to get that forgiveness. In pursuing this objective, I might try to seduce him. If that doesn't work, I might try to be pathetic and get his pity. I'll pursue each tactic until it becomes clear that it isn't working, and then I will switch to a new tactic.

At all times I'll pay close attention to my partner to see if I'm making any headway with my current tactic. Since all my efforts are focused on getting something from my partner, by playing objectives I guarantee that we will stay connected. Not only do I watch my partner to see if I'm getting what I want, but I adjust my next actions based on what *he* is doing. So, if I've just tried to seduce him and he belittles me, that's going to affect my next action. I may be so angry about him belittling me that I yell at him in the next moment—on paper, not the best choice, but compelling and recognizably human just the same.

At the same time all this is going on, my partner is pursuing his own objective. His will likely be completely different from mine. He may be trying to end our relationship, and his initial anger was the springboard he was using to get there. So, while I am trying to get his forgiveness, he is trying to break

Objectives keep you connected to your partner. You have to watch him closely to see if you're getting what you want.

up with me, and the resulting dynamic tension may produce a very interesting scene.

The pursuit of objectives is the heartbeat of theater. The audience watches with delight as the hero chases his goal, whether the hero is Hamlet, Pinocchio, or the goddess Diana. When the objective is clear, the audience becomes invested in the outcome of the story. And the audience's enjoyment increases with each new tactic. Half the fun happens when a character is using ludicrous tactics to get what he wants.

SWITCHING TACTICS

The only way objectives help scenes is if the improviser knows that she has to switch to a new tactic when the current one isn't working. In fact, the reason a lot of scenes get stuck is that the improviser stubbornly sticks to the same tactic (such as arguing) long after it has become clear that arguing isn't going to win the day.

I think most people would agree that it's important for improvisers to be changed in scenes. The difficulty is that we usually spend all our energy trying to get the *other guy* to change. Try adopting this mantra, "Let someone be changed. Let it be me." A bit corny perhaps, but you get the idea. In the middle of a scene, when I am heavily invested in my point of view (and perhaps think my character is only capable of that one point of view), it may be very difficult for me to find a way to change that seems believable. This is where switching tactics is a lifesaver (and scene-saver).

All I have to do is switch tactics and the energy of the scene will immediately move forward.

When first practicing objectives, most improvisers use talking as their main tactic. If I see that in class and say, "switch tactics," they usually start *talking* about something else. Tactics work best when they involve a range of choices: physical actions, emotional offers, status behaviors, and words.

To go back to our example scene, let's say I'm trying to achieve my objective of getting my husband's forgiveness, and I have chosen seduction as my tactic. Instead of standing at the kitchen sink and talking sexy to him, I might go over and sit on his lap, take off his coat, run my fingers through his hair, take off my clothes, etc.

The pursuit of objectives is the heartbeat of theater. The audience watches with delight as the hero chases his goal, whether the hero is Hamlet, Pinocchio, or the goddess Diana. When the objective is clear, the audience becomes invested in the outcome of the story.

Let someone be changed. Let it be YOU.

On the other hand, if my objective is to get him to pity me, I might pout or look dejected, or start to cry, or do any number of things that don't involve speaking. If I'm trying to provoke him to anger, I might slap him, slam doors, stare coldly at him, etc.

All the above-mentioned tactics are fairly logical and we can see how they might succeed. The fun comes when characters use ridiculous tactics to get their objectives. Just like in real life, when a situation is deteriorating and we have exhausted logical tactics, we start using illogical ones. I may be trying to get my husband's forgiveness, but if he makes me mad, I will probably yell at him.

Sometimes a character uses ridiculous tactics because he doesn't know any better. This is often the case in comic scenes. Someone trying to get a job as a waiter may end up doing a striptease or singing "Oklahoma," or crying, or hiding under the table—depending on the situation, all these might be plausible tactics he would use to pursue his objective.

Remember, if you're failing to achieve your objective, try a new tactic. If you've exhausted every logical tactic at your disposal, start trying *illogical* ones. Keep trying until you win or lose.

Tactics ripple outward from the logical to the ridiculous.

How Objectives Help End Scenes

Lots of scenes start strong, then peter out with no satisfying resolution. This situation can be avoided if somebody is playing an objective, because the scene will come to a natural resolution when the objective is either achieved or abandoned. Returning to our example scene, if I'm seeking my husband's forgiveness and he gives it and decides to stay with me, both our objective pursuits have come to a natural ending. I have achieved my objective, and he has not. The only thing left to do is to show the audience how we have been affected by the journey we have taken.

From the chapter on protagonist-based storytelling, you may have gotten the idea that the protagonist is the only one pursuing an objective. This isn't true. *Everyone in every scene should have something they're trying to attain.* In fact, the nonprotagonists in the scene may have objectives that run counter to the goal of the protagonist, forming some of the obstacles in the story. The protagonist's objective is usually the most prominent, and the protagonist is often successful. In our example

Everyone in every scene should be pursuing an objective.

scene, either the husband or the wife could be the protagonist, depending upon who had the most at stake.

The protagonist's objective is usually the most prominent.

Objective Drill

Now that you understand how objectives and tactics work, you can incorporate practice into your pre-show warm-up. In pairs, the improvisers start simple scenes. In each pair, Player A chooses an objective based on something that happens in the first moments of the interaction. She then proceeds to try a tactic, and her partner responds. Player A then either continues with that same tactic (if it seems to be working) or tries another one. Player B's only job is to respond. At first, Player B should respond normally. After a little while, he can respond in unexpected ways.

It's important that Player A keeps checking in to see if her tactics are working. Is she any closer to her original goal? If not, she should switch tactics and try again. Remember, it's important that tactics cover a range of behavior: physical action, emotional states, status, etc. The exercise ends when Player A either: 1) gets her goal, or 2) gives up.

The players then switch roles and Player B tries to achieve an objective. After both players have pursued objectives, they then play one more scene, with both people pursuing new objectives simultaneously. It's important that both players pay close attention to their partners, and let each new tactic be a response to the offer their partner just made.

WHEN YOU ACHIEVE YOUR OBJECTIVE TOO QUICKLY—OR NOT AT ALL

Objectives are sometimes achieved prematurely. This can happen for a variety of reasons. Often, acting from a hair-trigger "say yes" reflex, your partner may give you what you want right off the bat. Or you may be so darned compelling that you sweep him off his feet. In either case, you sense the scene isn't over. When this happens, you may need to pick a new objective—one that's a bit meatier, harder to achieve.

The reverse situation occurs when the scene has been going on for quite awhile, and you're no closer to your goal. If you're confident that you've been switching tactics and paying attention, maybe it's time to throw in the towel. In this case, it's likely that your partner has gotten stubborn about his own objective (which is probably the opposite of yours). All you need to do is let him win, and the scene will be over. Remember, even if you're the protagonist, the scene doesn't have to end with your success.

THE TRAP

Objectives and tactics are very powerful tools when used properly. The one trap of pursuing objectives is that we can become so single-minded about winning that we are only in *sending* mode. By this I mean that we make lots of offers and change our behavior, but our actions aren't in response to our partners'. To use objectives effectively, you must send and receive with equal enthusiasm. You must take in the offers of your partner and let them affect your journey. This makes improvising simpler, because you aren't having to "think up" anything. You are merely reacting to what your partner is doing, and letting it change your course.

Use the power for good. Send and receive with equal enthusiasm.

OBJECTIVES AS SCENE SAVERS

Establishing an objective can be a great way to clarify and energize a weak scene. Once you and your partners know that someone wants something, you can start to make connected offers that either enhance or impede that quest. It doesn't matter if nobody had an objective up to that point—the important thing is you've got one *now*—pursue it with vigor and the scene may be saved.

Objectives are mighty workhorses. They stimulate authentic human-style behavior on stage; they let the audience identify with your character; they create movement through a story; and they ensure you stay connected with (and motivated by) your partner. We all use them, all the time, so it's not even like learning a new skill; it's more a matter of reminding ourselves of what we already know. Human beings have strong desires and we're powerful fierce creatures when we go after them.

The How and Why of Where
Creating Environments

Most improvisers work on a nearly bare stage, with a few chairs, and perhaps a table or two. The audience keeps its attention on what it can see, unless you create a rich environment by making the invisible visible. Clearly defined environments (or "Wheres") benefit improvisers, too. They help us feel grounded in scenes, give us things to do when nerves take over, and generate narrative without our having to think. A strong Where can also evoke emotions in us, and increase the reality of the scene for us and for our audiences.

Creating environment goes beyond merely getting a location for a scene. The objects in locations have meaning and importance, as do the characters' *responses* to their environments. Since space-object work is one of the few improv skills you can practice by yourself, let's start with that.

SPACE OBJECTS

A space object is any object (invisible to the eye) which may come into play during a scene: a refrigerator, a pencil, an elephant, a racecar, a lamppost. Because the object is invisible, it's most "real" when the improviser is in contact with it. By

Clearly defined environments help us feel grounded in scenes, give us things to do when nerves take over, and present narrative choices without our having to think.

Space objects exist when we're using them, and begin to fade away the minute we stop.

that I mean that a space-object toothbrush is "visible" when the improviser is using it, but tends to evaporate when it's put down on the sink and the improviser walks away.

The audience will remember where things were placed in the room (much better than we do most of the time!). If a player pulls out a filing cabinet drawer and leaves it open, the audience will laugh if later in the scene another actor walks through it. But even the audience will see objects best when we're in contact with them.

Some thoughts on space objects:

- they have a specific size, shape, and weight
- they take up a certain amount of space in the world
- they may inspire emotional responses in us
- they may be utilitarian, commonplace, valuable or exotic
- as a general rule, they shouldn't fly around the room, vanish, or change shape for no reason

Here are some ways to practice your mime skills so you can become proficient in the use of space objects.

Solo Space-Object Drill

Practice with real objects. Pick up an actual newspaper and read a story on the front page. Then look through subsequent pages and scan the headlines of other stories. Now, put the paper down and repeat what you did, miming all the activities. If you get stuck and can't remember what you did at any point, pick up the actual paper and repeat the activity. Then put it down and mime it. Do this with as many things as you can think of. Cut carrots, drive your car, wash your hair, watch television, play the piano. When you are doing the actual activity, pay attention to things like size, weight, resistance, texture, etc. A pencil takes up a certain amount of space in your hand. A broom drags with a certain resistance over a smooth surface; the resistance would increase when sweeping a rough surface.

Practice *a lot* with doors. Which way does the door open? What kind of knob or handle does it have? Does it lock? When improvising, you'll probably use space-object doors more than any other object in the world. Get proficient!

One way to help your ensemble and the audience "see" what you're seeing is to identify the defining feature of the object. By defining feature, I mean the aspect of the object that lets us know it's a telephone and not a set of stereo headphones. Even with very clean space-object work, what you are doing will always be more obvious to you than to your partners. You *know* what you're doing—they're trying to guess by watching you; the defining feature will help them guess more accurately. Try this exercise.

Identify and use the defining feature of the object.

Defining Feature Drill

The players stand in a circle. The first player creates a space object and uses it. The other players guess what the object is and describe the defining feature that helped them recognize the object. It's very useful to know, for instance, when opening a package of bread to make a sandwich, that undoing the twist-tie and untwirling the bag helps make it clear that it's a bag of bread. Then, when the improviser reaches in and pulls out a slice, it's less likely that his partner will come in and say, "I see you bought another hamster."

You may notice that point of view is a critical factor in recognizing space objects. Players standing on either side of the improviser will usually have a much harder time seeing what the object is. The players across the circle (viewing it head on) usually have a much easier time. This is helpful to remember if you're in a scene and you've just created a brilliant submarine periscope and one of your partners (standing behind you or in the wings) comes in and calls it a ladder.

How can you avoid this problem? By *calling* it a periscope, or saying that you can see the destroyer bearing down on you. Be very overt with your offers, especially when it's important to the scene that your partners understand what you're doing. Unless your space-object work is superb, don't rely on your mime skills alone to carry the day. (In any event, don't forget that the greatest skill you can possess is the ability to laugh it off when everything goes wrong on stage. Don't get all in a twist about a missed space-object offer.)

When you're practicing, always picture the object before you start to use it—and make sure you see the object in specific detail. If you're going to pick up a space-object hairbrush, see it first. Is it large or small, plastic or wood? Does it have natural bristles? Is it an heirloom from your grandmother, or a cheap brush you got for free when you bought hairspray? Picturing the object in detail before touching it will help you be more specific in using it. That heirloom brush from Grandma will probably get treated more carefully than the freebie.

Some objects affect us emotionally. While you may not get too worked up about that stapler you stole from your office two years ago, a photograph of your first love is likely to inspire a reaction in you. If we can incorporate that idea when we improvise, space objects will not simply be mimed hand props we use to fill out the scene, but may become central offers. And since we are on the lookout for ways to increase our emotional commitment in scenes, this is a great place to start.

In order for space objects to have an impact on us, we have to take an extra moment to really see the object and let our imaginations supply an emotional response. When you're practicing on your own with space objects, vary their importance. Make sure some of them are everyday items, and that some of them are more significant. Practice with real objects of significance to you—how do you hold an important object? How do you treat an object that is fragile or expensive? Think back to the Hot Object exercise in chapter 4. Remember how you handled your important object? The way you felt when you looked at it?

When creating space objects, remember to move a little slower than you think you need to, and make your motions crisper than usual. In real life, when I am picking up a glass, I simply move my fingers into a clamp until they make contact with the glass. The glass stops my fingers from moving too far. With space-object glasses, there's nothing to stop your fingers except your paying attention. While in real life you may grab a door handle sloppily and push the door closed, on stage you will need to make those separate and distinct motions with as much attention to detail as possible.

If you allow space objects to affect you emotionally, they will not simply be mimed props, but may generate narrative offers in the scene.

By carefully observing, studying, and reproducing our everyday interactions with objects, our scene work will become more specific, believable and evocative.

Creating Wheres

The term "Wheres" is used broadly in improv and can have several meanings. The most obvious is that of location: Is the scene taking place in a grocery store, on a tropical island, or in a prison cell? *Where* work also includes less tangible aspects of environment, such as temperature (or weather), humidity, light sources, etc. The improviser is also responsible for showing the character's *relationship to his environment*. Does the location conjure up feelings of safety or danger, welcome or rejection, normalcy or nightmare? As you immerse yourself in environments, you'll begin to experience the power of being affected by place and circumstance. Here's an exercise to help you practice not only seeing an environment, but also being *affected* by it.

First create the environment and then express your relationship to it.

Imagination Walk

This is a guided visualization performed with your eyes open. Each player should find a place in the room to work—you won't be interacting with each other; rather, you'll be creating your own individual environment. You'll need someone to act as the leader, calling out the instructions. The leader should go slowly enough to allow the improvisers time to really explore each aspect of the exercise. If you are leading, you'll get a sense of pace by watching the improvisers closely. The following is the basic script the leader will use. There are any number of variations—feel free to take liberties! Try to incorporate all of the senses: touch, sight, smell, sound, taste.

- You're standing in front of a door of some kind. Look at the door carefully. What material is it made of? What is the texture of the door? How large is it? Reach out and touch it.
- You see the way the door works. Open the door, paying attention to which way it moves.

- Go through the door into the room beyond. Make a mental note of the location of the door.
- You find yourself in an ice cream parlor. What's the temperature in the room? Is the air dry or humid? How does the room smell?
- You hear something and you pay attention to it until you figure out what it is.
- Look around the room. On one wall, you see a sign listing the flavors. Go over and look at the sign.
- You can see the ice cream from where you are standing. Move closer, and decide what you will order.
- The server gives you your ice cream. Take a taste. Let it sit on your tongue. Feel its coolness in your mouth. As you eat your ice cream, walk around the room a bit.
- There are some other customers in the ice cream parlor. How are they dressed? Look down at your own clothing. What are you wearing?
- You notice a sign on the opposite wall that you didn't see before. What does it say?
- Look at the light in the room. Is it man-made or natural light?
- Look down at the floor. What is it made of or covered with?
- You finish your ice cream and walk back toward the door.
- Open the door and go back out the way you came in; you are now standing where you started.
- Look at the door once again. You see something this time that you didn't notice before. What is it?
- As you turn to walk away, notice if the temperature is different than it was inside. Is the light different? How are you feeling?

After you finish the exercise, talk about what you experienced. This exercise is often very rich and brings up all sorts of unexpected reactions in people. Ask the following questions to generate discussion:

- What did you notice about the exercise?
- Did you have any emotions come up during the exercise? When?
- Did things you saw surprise you?
- What kind of door did you have?
- Was it easy or hard to see things?
- What time period were you in? Did this surprise you?
- Were there any inconsistencies in the place? How did you deal with these?

This exercise gives us a chance to practice letting our imaginations lead us. Our creative minds will supply endless details if we make the space for it to happen. Because the exercise is silent, the improvisers are free to follow their bodies and their creativity. In this exercise, the conscious mind can be made to submit to the will of the imagination, as the improviser sees each new element and incorporates it into an unconscious story. Improvisers often comment on how quickly new elements come into "view," and on the responses that different elements created in them. For example, in a recent class, an improviser was having a perfectly lovely time in a 1950s ice cream parlor until he noticed a sign that read "Whites Only—No Coloreds Allowed." He then felt terrible and wanted to leave the place as quickly as possible. He told us the feeling was instantaneous and quite surprising in its strength.

In this example, the leader has chosen a specific location (ice cream parlor). The exercise can also be more open-ended if the leader uses generalized language. For instance, after the players have walked through the door, the leader might say, "You have entered the next place. Look around you . . ." Many times, the spaces the improvisers see aren't traditional rooms at all, and they have a wonderful time exploring the spaces created solely by their imaginations.

The value of using specific locales is that it forces the players to make adjustments as the leader adds new information. This approximates what happens in scenes, when our partners

Our imaginations will supply endless details if we make the space for it to happen.

are adding disparate offers that we must incorporate into the reality we have created in our minds.

This is one of the best benefits of the exercise—it helps us see that we can make seemingly unconnected elements work together, if we are flexible enough and open to changing our ideas. I call this "knitting," and it's a great skill to have in all aspects of improvising. In Where work in particular, improvisers can get stuck if they think an element they have added to the scene is at odds with what's already in place. The Imagination Walk illustrates that a lot of different ideas or offers can be made to work together. Creating a Where by yourself is one thing; adding other improvisers into the mix is another. The following exercise will give you practice doing this with partners.

If you stay relaxed you can make seemingly unconnected elements work together in any environment.

Location Round Robin

In this exercise, players create Wheres together without speaking. Two players start a scene without a suggestion. One player starts with an activity that suggests a location, such as pulling bread out of an oven. The second player performs another activity that would take place in the same environment, like kneading dough. After both players have physically engaged with the environment, they may speak and proceed with the scene. It's not necessary for the improvisers to do the entire scene—you're practicing *starting* scenes. When the next two improvisers begin, they don't have to assume the positions of the first two—they should start from nothing.

When we improvise, most of us stop our activity the minute we open our mouths. This may be due to the fact that we have enough to worry about in making verbal offers. But one of the great things about space-object work is that we can learn how to *talk less* and *do more*. And a fully realized environment can help create narrative offers, as we'll see in a bit. Make sure that when you start talking, you don't stop your activity. Your goal is to become adept at using space objects and carrying on with the rest of the scene.

Space-object work helps us TALK less and DO more.

In life, if I'm washing the dishes and my husband and I are chatting, I don't necessarily stop washing dishes to do so. If something really important comes up, I will probably stop, dry my hands, and turn to give him my full attention. But if we're just shooting the breeze, I will likely continue with my activity. And even if I stop for a moment, I will probably resume my activity at some point in our conversation.

Sometimes two improvisers will begin a scene simultaneously, making disparate offers. What should you do then? The following exercise is wonderful for showing how to make the most of this opportunity.

Dueling Offers

This exercise was inspired by the work of Kirk Livingston. The exercise is played without suggestions from the audience.

Round One: The players may speak during the exercise. Two players get up. Player A makes a Where offer by performing an activity. Player B engages in an activity that fits in with the first offer. They start a scene. They then start a new scene; this time Player B makes the first Where offer.

Round Two: Both players start simultaneous activities without paying attention to each other. They continue their activities as they check in visually to see what their partner is doing. The first verbal offer should make sense of both activities, without referring to them.

I saw a great example of this in a recent class. Player A was making a rather large sandwich. Player B was preparing a patient for surgery. The first verbal offer was from Player B, who said, "Doctor, we need to get started." Player A, without missing a beat, grasped the sandwich between his teeth and walked over to where the space-object patient was lying. As he started surgery, he kept eating. It was lovely! This worked because Player B trusted that Player A would make use of her offer.

I love this exercise because it teaches us to expand our thinking. So many scenes suffer from literalism—thinking that everything has to be normal or believable. For my money, it's much more fun to have a surgeon eating a sandwich with one hand and performing an operation with the other than it is to watch an improviser try to imitate real surgery. And the situation has all sorts of comic possibilities built into it.

Earlier I talked about how Where work can facilitate narrative. I saw a scene set in a coffeehouse that catered to bikers. Two tourists had unknowingly seated themselves on the favorite couch of the meanest, most dangerous biker in the gang. The male tourist was (happily enough) a low-status, sensitive, non-aggressive guy. When the biker started chasing him around the coffeehouse, the tourist ran behind the counter and started looking frantically through the cupboards for something with which to defend himself. The improviser opened a cupboard and (as he told us after the scene), he suddenly "saw" a coffee bean grinder sitting on the shelf. He grabbed it, and started spewing ground coffee beans in the biker's face. It was a very fulfilling scene.

One of the most satisfying things about the scene as a whole was that much of the story was created physically, or through the use of environmental offers. When the tourists first arrived at the coffeehouse, they discovered it was a biker hangout because of the magazines lying on the tables. When the chase scene began, the improvisers all worked together to create a sense of place through the physical offers they made.

A strong Where can lend a sense of cohesion to a scene. In the example above, if the improvisers had just stood and shouted at each other, it's likely that the offers would have gotten further and further away from the first reality. The tourist might have suddenly remembered that he had an AK-47 in his backpack, which would have been a big letdown, as it would have destroyed the internal logic of the scene. Searching for a weapon *in the context of the environment* made the discovery of the weapon an important part of the scene; moreover, the coffee grinder underscored the basic comic premise of the scene, which was the anomaly of a coffeehouse for bikers.

In the example of the sandwich-eating surgeon, it would have been very satisfying if he had drunk water or saline solution out of the I.V. drip, or patched a wound with a piece of lettuce from his sandwich. Having the scene take place in a particular location opens up all kinds of possibilities without our having to think too much. When we practice using our imaginations to see rich environments, offers arise with much greater ease.

GROUPS OF MORE THAN TWO

As with everything else, Where work gets trickier the more people you have on stage. Here are some tips to simplify the process.

- The more people in a scene, the cleaner the space-object work has to be.
- In a group scene, back up your physical space-object offers with verbal nametags (e.g., "lower the periscope")
- If you're adding a new space object to a scene in progress, make a sound effect to draw the attention of your partners to your offer.

Group Location Exercise

Two improvisers start a scene from nothing and create an environment using space objects. The improvisers may speak as well. More players enter the scene, with each player adding a new element to the location. When doing this, the players take care to make a sound effect for each new offer. For example, in a scene set in a jewelry store, the first two players might show us the front door (with a little bell that rings each time the door is opened) and the front jewelry counter (which squeaks slightly when the actors lean on it).

The next player in might be a new customer, who goes to yet another counter (of course, the bell rings when this new customer comes into the shop). Another player might arrive from the bank to pick up the cash from the safe. Since a safe may prove to be a big offer in the scene, it's important that this player make it very clear what she is doing, using sound effects to draw attention to her physical offers.

All the improvisers in the scene should be talking as little as possible and focusing their energies on making note of all the offers being made. Then the scene continues, using the location as it has been created.

In a group scene, draw attention to your space-object offers with sound effects or verbal nametags ("lower the periscope").

It's very satisfying to the audience to see more than one player use the same object. I once saw a very funny roommate scene in which one player, Holly, was moving out due to ongoing disputes with her housemate, Lisa. Holly returned to get the last of her belongings. Lisa made it clear that she didn't trust Holly and accompanied her through the house to make sure she didn't steal anything. As Holly proceeded through the house, she passed through several doors, which she opened and closed behind her. Lisa opened and closed each door in exactly the same way. After arriving in the rear of the house (the bedroom), Holly suddenly stole something and started running back through the house. This chase scene was delightful because both players had such a good time with all the doors they had created at the beginning of the scene. This took a lot of concentration on the part of the players, and it reaped huge rewards.

Beyond Locations – How to Create Environments

A lot of improv scenes occur no place in particular, at no particular time of day. Two, three, or more improvisers stand (or sit) and talk, and eventually the lights go down. Often, location is designated only by a verbal offer, such as, "This is sure a nice restaurant you have here." One of the things that sets theatrical improvisation apart from bar-prov is that we have the time and space to create a richer visual picture for our audiences.

The best way to create visual pictures is through physical offers. Merely stating you're in a restaurant will give the audience only the barest sense of place. If, on the other hand, you and your partners let us see that this is the world's tiniest restaurant, with narrow walls and only one table, now we have a much better sense of place, and a heightened sense of anticipation about how that environment is going to be used. This really takes the pressure off having to "think up" funny offers. Just moving around in this space will be funny. This is true of dramatic scenes as well. For instance, if a prisoner of war is being questioned in a forbidding cell, the sense of tension will be greater than if he is in a big, comfy room. (Or worse yet, no place in particular.)

A lot of improv scenes occur no place in particular, at no particular time of day. When the audience sees a clearly established environment, there's a heightened sense of anticipation about how that environment will be used.

Environment Tag

Two improvisers play a silent scene from nothing. Their goal is to create a sense of place that has to do with weather, light, time of day, indoor/outdoor location, etc. This could involve sound effects, physical offers, emotional responses to place, and so on. After the scene has progressed enough to have a sense of place and environment, the players stop and two more players start a new scene.

For example, to create a scene in an unexplored jungle, the improvisers might hack their way through the underbrush, and show us the heat and humidity by wiping their foreheads or pulling sticky clothing away from their bodies. They can show us their fear of the unknown, whether or not they have enough supplies, and aspects of their relationship, all without speaking a single word. While the improvisers are engaged in these activities, they will be immersing themselves further into the reality of the scene, which will help deepen their offers and connect them more fully to their characters.

Similarly, players can create a snowball fight between young children and let us see if it's snowing softly or if the children are about to be caught in a blizzard; we can get a sense of their ages and abilities. Offers like these increase the audience's investment in the scene because they are not simply being told these things are so; they are *seeing* them, which increases the sense of reality of the scene.

At first it may seem daunting to try to convey all this information without speaking. It's really simply a matter of practice. And, like the space-object work, the first step to creating a rich environment is to see it before you. Secondly, you must give yourself a chance to react to what you see. If you see a hot, steamy jungle before you, it's easy to feel your clothes sticking to you and the sweat running down the back of your shirt.

The first step to creating a rich environment is to see it in front of you.

Creating environments in this way is also a good incentive to keep in visual connection with your partner. As each of you is making physical offers, the other will want to be as tuned in as possible. You'll also be able to see subtle facial expressions that may give a sense of emotion, relationship, status, etc.

Environment and Status

Status can play a huge part in creating a rich environment. By showing how the character reacts to the space he's in, we give the audience important information about the scene. Here we will focus on status as it relates to place.

If I have been having terrible headaches and am now sitting in a specialist's office, waiting for the results of a brain tumor test, I will probably play low status to my environment. This means I'll be submitting to the environment emotionally and behaviorally. For instance, I'm likely to be sitting quietly, not touching anything on the walls or desk. I may peruse a magazine to calm my nerves, but I am likely to treat it with care, replacing it where I found it, or possibly even straightening up the other magazines on the table as I do so. My reaction to the space is likely to be apprehensive and tense.

On the other hand, if I'm in my own home on a Sunday morning, I am much more likely to play high status to my environment. I may scuffle around oblivious to my surroundings (since I know them so well). As I read the Sunday paper, I may toss it all over the floor around me. I may flop down on the couch and put my feet up on the coffee table. Being in this environment may give me a great sense of peace and comfort.

You can probably see how incorporating status and emotional relationships to space will enhance and deepen scene work. By combining these elements with space-object work, your imagination can kick into high gear, and will start spitting out all sorts of narrative offers, too.

Solo Status Scenes

In this exercise, improvisers take turns playing silent solo scenes in specific locations. These scenes are very short. When teaching, I time the scenes, and limit them to one minute. This helps lower the freakout factor, and encourages the improvisers to get to the heart of the work as quickly as possible. It's helpful to have a list of locations handy. You may also want to assign a character, for example, "You're a young man in the draft office of the army in 1971." Or, "You are an old woman at the graveside of your husband." You can also give only the location as a suggestion, and let each improviser choose who they are playing. (See Appendix B for suggestions.)

The improviser takes a moment to visualize the environment, then shows us as much as she can without speaking. In the graveside example, ideally, we would see the following:

- the character's status to the graveyard (and to the gravesite): high status and proud, or disdainful, low status and reverent or frightened, etc.
- whether or not other people are present
- the character's emotional state
- the time of year
- the time of day
- the air temperature, humidity; light conditions
- the character's emotional relationship to her dead husband

When making up the list of locations, be sure to include some places that suggest both high- and low-status possibilities. It's also interesting to suggest places that seem status neutral, and let the improviser create the status relationship. I've often been delightfully surprised by unexpected choices in this exercise. For example, for a high-status player, I suggested the following: "You are a grown man who was disowned years ago by your wealthy father. You have been summoned home and are waiting to see him in his den." Although this improviser started the scene high status (as usual), when his eye fell on a picture of his family over the mantle, he softened and the most wonderful change came over him. He began to lovingly explore the mementos in his father's office as if reclaiming his lost childhood. It was a very moving scene, and completely believable. And the whole thing only lasted one minute. Because of the actor's emotional commitment to the place, we were invested in him without even knowing the details of the situation. If the scene had continued on to include his father, we would have been keenly interested to see their relationship unfold.

If you know that you tend to play high status all the time, practice these solo scenes with an emphasis on being low status (or vice versa). It's sometimes easier to relinquish our favorite status roles to places than to people. After you become comfortable playing a range of status behaviors, you can branch out to include human partners.

If you're stuck in a rut, always playing the same status, try playing the opposite status in relation to your environment. Sometimes it's easier to relinquish our favorite roles to places than to people.

Stretching Your Where Vocabulary

This is a great, quick warm-up game to help open up the imagination. When we first start doing location scenes, I've noticed that improvisers often create Wheres based on other improv scenes they've seen set in the same location. So, most beach scenes start with someone laying out a beach towel and putting on suntan lotion. Most café scenes start with two people being seated at a table and given menus. This next drill lets us go beyond what we've seen in other scenes.

Verbal Warm-up – Wheres

Improvisers stand or sit in a circle. Someone suggests a location, such as "beach." The players make verbal offers of things that might be found in that location. The offers are made randomly; more than one person may be speaking at a time. Try to listen to your partners' offers and let a free-association begin—in other words, let your partners' offers add to or even change what you are seeing in your mind's eye.

This exercise helps expand our imaginations. For instance, the location "beach" led to the following suggestions in a recent rehearsal: moonlight, a locked-up lifeguard tower, a homeless person asleep on the sand, seagull tracks, trash cans, a couple making love, dolphins offshore, distant music coming from a radio, and a child's sand bucket and shovel, abandoned at the water's edge. This was a revelation: an improv beach with no beach towels, sunshine, or suntan lotion!

When practicing, be sure that some of your starting suggestions are typical improv locations, and that some are more exotic and unusual. This is a great exercise to do before a show, to open up everyone's imaginations and to practice building on each other's ideas.

Using the Stage Creatively

Improvising in a theater, we have the opportunity to create multi-layered environments. We aren't bound by the constraints of television or film, in which each scene takes place in only one location at a time. One of the great strengths of theater is its ability to represent different states of consciousness, time, and space. We can see the internal workings of a character's mind at the same time we are watching that character in a scene. We can create multiple locales on the same stage, and direct the audience's attention to them as the scene progresses.

Split Focus Scenes

Split focus scenes involve several improvisers creating different places on the stage at the same time. For example, two improvisers may be hiking through the woods on one side of the stage. On the other side, two more improvisers have created a ranger's station, where concerned parents have come to seek help finding their children who went hiking and haven't been seen in several days.

The focus of the scene shifts back and forth between these two locations, and more locations may be added. In order for split focus scenes to be satisfying, two things must happen: the improvisers must listen closely to all the offers being made (and try to incorporate the offers from the other locale), and the players must keep the realities of each location clear and distinct.

Here's an example of the first skill. If we're watching the lost hikers scene, the dialogue might sound like this:

Ranger: Well, ma'am, you were right to come in. These woods are very dangerous this time of year, because the baby bears are just starting to explore and the mothers are pretty protective of their cubs.

Hiker 1: [*Lost in the woods*] Did you hear that noise? Maybe it's something we could catch and eat!

Mother: [*At ranger's station*] Are my children safe?

Ranger: Well, they'll probably be fine, as long as they don't go anywhere near a cub or its mother.

Hiker 2: You go around that way, and we'll try to corner it.

The fun for the audience comes from having information that the hikers don't have; it's also a fairly simple scene to play, because all the players are taking turns contributing to the narrative. It might continue like this:

Hiker 1: [*Moving slowly through the underbrush*] My mom is such a worry wart. She thinks I can't do anything right, like she has to follow me everywhere and take care of me.

Mother: Oh, dear, my son's an idiot—I don't think he'll have the sense to stay away from a bear cub!

Hiker 2: [*Crouching down in the clearing, picking up a stick*] Yeah, my mom's the same way. You'd think that they could see we're old enough to take care of ourselves . . .

Split focus scenes require a different kind of listening and also an awareness that you are playing in a two-person scene with your partner-in-locale, but you are really in a four-person scene. Therefore, you will speak one-quarter of the time (at most), and will be listening and responding non-verbally the rest of the time.

When the focus is on the other locale, you can either go into a soft freeze or limit your offers to very subtle mimed interactions. Whatever you choose, make sure you can listen to the offers of the other players. You also want to be sure that whatever you're doing doesn't pull focus from the main action. It's not necessary for the lights to come down on each locale as the focus shifts; in fact, it's more interesting for the audience to be able to look back and forth between the two. Also, the quicker and smoother the transitions between players, the better, and using lights to shift focus will slow down the transition process.

Sometimes the two realities will merge. In our hiker example, the ranger and the mother may set out to find the hikers, or the hikers may find their way to the ranger's station. Other locations may be added as dictated by the story.

Split focus scenes require a different kind of listening. You must listen to your own scene as well as the scene in the other locale.

Split Levels

In addition to split focus scenes set in multiple locales, we can create a single locale with separate areas. If we're doing a scene set in a Victorian mansion, we might have an entryway, drawing room, kitchen, and library which occupy the stage throughout the scene. If these separate areas are on different levels (real or imagined), we have created a much richer stage picture for our audience.

It's ideal if your stage has actual platforms, stairs, chairs, or troughs that create different levels. But *imagined* levels may also exist on the same plane on stage (in fact, there's an entire play based on this idea: Alan Ayckbourne's *Taking Steps*). In our Victorian mansion, the entryway and drawing room may be on the "main floor," with the kitchen downstairs and the library "upstairs." The first improviser to use those spaces should take care to be crisp with their physical offers. If we are lucky, the players will all move from one level to another in the course of the scene, doing their best to mimic the paths of the stairways.

Levels add dimension to all kinds of scenes, and help change the perspective of the scene in progress. Split level areas can also help the momentum and pace of the scene as the action moves from one place to another.

Split Level Practice

Two improvisers start a scene (either from a suggestion or from nothing). These players establish one area in a larger location, and continue the scene. As more players enter the scene, they add levels to the location (upstairs, downstairs, etc.), and continue the narrative of the scene. Pay attention to *direction* when practicing. By that I mean that if someone's on the upstairs landing calling down to me in the entry hall, they should be looking down and I should be looking up. Only in this way will the illusion hold up. This can be challenging, because our tendency is to look into the eyes of the person who's speaking to us. When you're practicing this skill, put your focus on the physical environment, and on keeping the illusion alive.

After you've had a chance to practice for awhile, make sure you use all the areas in the locale. Get used to going up and down space-object stairs, ladders, trees, gangways, etc. Have fun connecting physically with your environment.

Scenes Set in One Locale

This works well in rehearsal and performance. Start with a suggestion of a location that would have smaller locations contained within it, such as: castle, municipal buildings, monastery, school, forest, etc. Then do a series of scenes that take place in different parts of the location. (This differs from the split-level practice in that scenes take place in only one location at a time. For instance, if our suggestion is "school," one scene might take place in the principal's office, the next in the boiler room, etc.) Place your focus on creating each Where in detail: the room, objects, activities of each place should be distinct. Let the Where inform your choice of character, attitude, emotion, etc.

This structure gives us a jumping-off point, and I especially like it because each scene starts with life already in progress. Characters tend to know one another, work or play together, and are invested in their activities. It's fun for an audience, too, as they watch us create each new area in the location. When asking for suggestions, it's helpful to give the audience an example (so you can avoid getting the same location over and over again). I might say, "May I have a location that would contain several smaller locations? For instance, an amusement park." This helps us avoid doing too many Disneyland scenes.

Space objects, locations, and environments transform scenes from two dimensions into three. In a fully realized scene, the audience will be as affected and moved by the invisible world as they are by the visible one. If we're in the business of engaging each other at a heart level, a gut level, we'll need to spend as much energy on our external circumstances as we do on our internal experiences. And improvising is much easier when you can see and feel your surroundings. Less thinking, more *being*.

In a fully realized scene, the audience will be as affected and moved by the invisible world as they are by the visible one.

Notes

Get Off My Foot
Group Scenes

When the stage is filled with improvisers, one might think we'd have such merrymaking as has not been seen in many a day. Alas! As often as not a stage filled with improvisers more closely resembles a caffeine addicts' convention or (worse) a morose, uncomfortable, mass of humanity rooted to the stage like prisoners chained to a post.

In the interest of variety, shows need large group scenes, but the trouble lies with the math. Simple addition of actors causes nonlinear growth in complexity. A four-person scene isn't twice as complicated as a two-person scene, it's more like twelve times as complicated. The good news is that you can learn how to make group scenes sizzle. In this chapter we'll look at some ways to be fruitful as you multiply.

IDENTIFY A CENTRAL PROTAGONIST

A group scene with a central protagonist will be better than one without, because everyone on stage will know whose story is being told, and how they fit into that story. The great thing about the protagonist-centered structure is that everyone can play his or her parts with full abandon. Having a central

A group scene will be better if you establish a central protagonist.

figure for the story is very freeing, particularly in a group scene, because once you've caught on to the process, you will know when to speak, when to move, and when to be silent and still.

Protagonist-centered stories are discussed in detail in chapter 9; here we'll focus on how to establish a protagonist when more than two people are on stage.

The basic idea is still the same: near the beginning of the scene, it should become clear that one character has more at stake than the others do. That character will be our hero. But if there are six of you on stage, how can you know who that will be? (Well, in the first place, why are there six of you on stage? That's too many. Start with four.) The protagonist may be suggested by the physical grouping at the top of the scene, before anyone has even spoken. Let's say that the lights go down, the lights come up, and three of you are arranged in a semicircle around the fourth player. That grouping suggests that the person in the center is the protagonist, for three reasons. The most basic reason is that three of you are providing focus to the fourth. Second, the odd man out is often the protagonist, because that grouping suggests an underdog situation. Presumably, the three other characters feel powerful as a unit, and the odd man out will have to struggle to gain acceptance or freedom or whatever. Lastly, in this sort of grouping, we have a clump of three people and a single individual. Clumps are rarely protagonists. It will be much easier to convince the audience that an individual has the most at stake—provided the clump knows its job, and stays a clump (more on this in a bit).

In this example, we have a leg up because the physical grouping has suggested a protagonist. Let's assume the improvisers paid attention to that, and that the isolated individual (Player A) was endowed as the protagonist. We're not out of the woods yet, because there are three other people on stage who, if careless, could hijack the protagonist position away from its rightful owner. The job of the three non-protagonists is to deepen the hero's story, and to make sure all their offers stay centered on that story. One of the three may end up being an out-and-out villain. Another may prove to be the spiritual guide or friend to the hero and the third may help push the story forward while maintaining a neutral relationship with the protagonist.

But what if the first physical grouping doesn't suggest a central figure? Then the protagonist will have to be established some other way, probably with a verbal offer. Let's suppose the lights go down, the lights come up, and four of you are standing in a row facing out to the audience, and you are all equidistant from one another. Let's further suppose that one player makes an offer that you are on an assembly line in a factory. If all four players are doing their jobs equally well, exhibiting a similar emotional investment, you will not have a protagonist. Now it will be up to one of you (or a fifth player, entering from offstage) to endow *someone* on the line as being different. This can be done in any number of ways. One of you may suddenly have an emotional outburst, or stop working, or get promoted, or fired, or receive a telegram about bad news back home in Indiana. It doesn't matter what differentiates you as long as you get differentiated. Once you have established the protagonist, the story can proceed with some clarity.

Earlier I mentioned the idea of hijacking the protagonist's role. This happens a lot in group scenes, usually by accident. Let's say the story so far is that Billy, our hero, is trying to save his family business from bankruptcy. He has gone to the bank to ask hard-hearted old Mr. Wilkins to reconsider foreclosing on the factory. In this scene, Mr. Wilkins must take care not to become more sympathetic (or to have more at stake) than Billy. If we find out that Mr. Wilkins is in danger of losing his job, and his wife is very, very ill—everyone on stage (and in the audience) is going to be confused about whom the story will be about from this point on.

So Mr. Wilkins has two challenges: remaining unsympathetic, and enhancing *Billy's* story, by simply saying "No," or by adding more information that makes us root harder for Billy. He can also do or say anything to make Billy's life harder. The offers he makes should be about *Billy*, not about himself. If the improviser playing Mr. Wilkins has fun being a greedy, small-minded banker, Billy will probably still be the protagonist when he ends this transaction.

Providing Focus for the Audience

In a two-person scene, the audience tends to look back and forth, like spectators at a tennis match. In a group scene, there are a lot of places the audience might look, and all the players in a group scene are responsible for helping the audience in this regard. Having a clear stage picture plays a strong part here. This means if we have a Joan of Arc scene, and it's the big climactic moment when Joan gives her speech, everybody on stage should be arranged in such a way to focus all the attention on Joan. This might mean literally turning your body slightly toward her, reducing or eliminating any extraneous movement, and it certainly means being silent.

That example is pretty obvious. In the middle of stories, it may not seem so clear. As you begin to understand the rhythm of scenes, and how hero journeys unfold, you will start to have a sixth sense about where the focus needs to move. The focus should stay on the most important story element. Many times, that will be provided by the protagonist. But there will be other moments where the focus will be elsewhere. We may see the villain plotting against the protagonist; there may be a scene in which information is laid out by neutral parties that the protagonist isn't privy to; there may be a scene where we're simply getting to know other characters in the story. As long as the offers have to do with the central story, we won't get into a jam.

Remember: group scenes need focus. Regardless of how many people are onstage, the audience can only watch one interaction at a time. Each interaction may involve two people, or twenty (with a central focus). But you *don't* want two interactions occurring simultaneously.

STAY, GO, OR RIDE ALONG

It's easy to find yourself stuck on stage after making a perfectly lovely offer that helped the scene, and now you have no idea how to get offstage. The easiest way is to simply leave. So, if you have entered the scene playing the press secretary to the president, make your offer and leave again. You don't have to become a central figure. If you're needed again later you can come back.

There is one type of ancillary character who may indeed stay on stage during the whole scene, and that is a passenger. A passenger is a sort of fly on the wall, an audience surrogate who witnesses a transaction, but who will not necessarily enter the transaction directly. A passenger may be the movie patron in the row behind the protagonist and his girlfriend. It may be a

Group scenes need focus. Regardless of how many people are on stage, the audience can only watch one interaction at a time.

person at the next table in the café. Passengers are different from atmosphere players. Passengers pay attention to the main interaction, and may even react to it (usually silently), while atmosphere players are simply rounding out the scene. In a café scene, several improvisers may be playing the other patrons (who remain oblivious to the interaction), but a passenger, usually a lone individual, will be involved in the interaction, at least as an observer.

Here's a tip about playing atmosphere: don't get so involved in what you're doing that you stop listening to the offers in the scene. I was in a scene once, playing atmosphere in a nightclub, and I became so engrossed in my mimed conversation with my partner that I didn't hear the offer that a bomb had been planted in the club. When the sound effect of the bomb happened, I was still calmly drinking my Mai-Tai while everyone else was flying around and getting maimed. Not only did I miss all the fun, but also I ruined the reality of the scene.

How to Clump Effectively

As mentioned earlier, clumps of people can help us sense who the protagonist is by a process of elimination. But beyond that, clumps serve several important functions. Clumps help focus the audience's attention. Clumps can provide interesting stage pictures, adding depth and dimension and demarcating different playing areas.

To clump effectively, one has to develop an awareness of where everyone is on stage, what the main focus of the action is and how one fits into the larger whole. Early on in my teaching career, I was watching a barnyard scene that involved several pigs who, out of a keen sense of self-preservation, were plotting to overthrow the farmer. During a meeting of the pigs, all the improvisers were on their hands and knees in a horrible knot in the center of the stage, mostly facing away from the audience. I found myself directing, "Pigs! Arrange yourselves attractively!" From that moment on, whenever there was a group scene with an awkward stage picture, someone would invariably call out, "Pigs! Arrange yourselves attractively!"

Stage pictures can be symmetrical or asymmetrical, depending upon what's called for. Generally speaking, symmetrical groupings imply formality (such as two guards standing on

If you're providing atmosphere, don't get so involved in what you're doing that you stop listening to the offers in the scene.

either side of the king's throne), while asymmetrical groupings imply informality (such as an angry mob rushing to kill the monster). An attractive clump in an informal setting usually consists of groups of different sizes placed about the stage in random distances from the action and each other.

The Clump as Protagonist

Once in awhile, we will have what I call a "protagonist clump." This is usually two improvisers (although I've seen it happen with three or more) who fill the function of a single character, as in the example of Hansel and Gretel. These characters aren't really distinguishable from each other, and roughly the same adventures happen to both of them. They take turns being dumb, they are both in the same jam, and they both get rescued at the same time.

If you have a scene where the protagonist has been a clump for awhile, don't differentiate between them. Instead, the players should think "Hansel and Gretel," and behave as a unit.

The way to avoid protagonist clumps (which aren't as effective as single protagonists) is to make sure the characters are differentiated at the beginning of the scene. If there are two brothers whose mother has just died, *make it more important to one of them than the other*. It's harder to show how a clump has been affected by something, harder for clumps to make decisions, take action, etc.

When a Clump is the Perfect Choice

It's great to have a clump of secondary characters. Since three is such a strong storytelling and comedic number, three of something is often more satisfying than one. If you have a scene with a bumbling cop (who's not the protagonist), three bumbling cops are even more fun. Ditto paramedics, schoolchildren, astronauts, podiatrists, etc. For certain story elements, you have to have a clump or the scene won't work. Can you imagine a "kill the monster" mob scene with only two people yelling "Kill the monster?" (Actually, now that I think about it, that could be really funny.)

When a clump is called for, play it with vigor but remember this: if, in addition to the clump, there are two other main

Sometimes we have a protagonist clump. This is two or more improvisers who fill the function of a single character.

If you have a clump of two identical ancillary characters, make it three instead.

characters, the clump isn't going to be talking very often. In a two-person scene, each person may speak about 50 percent of the time; in a standard four-person scene, less than 25 percent of the time, because the protagonist will be the focus a lot of the time. In a *clump* scene, you may hardly speak at all, and most of your contributions to the scene may be physical, emotional, or mimed offers.

Each individual in a clump may differentiate themselves slightly from each other, but care should be taken that the overall impression is of a unit. In some instances (such as a Greek chorus), there should be no differentiation at all.

Group scenes can be a blast. A stage full of improvisers holds the promise of movement, momentum, and mayhem. All we have to do is harness the power. When we focus the energy of the group on a central idea, we bring the story and the stage to life.

Clumps don't talk much.

Notes

14
It Ain't Just Window Dressing
The Essence of Genres

It's a dark and stormy night. In the mist, a lonely-looking castle beckons the traveling salesman who has lost his way. Standing at the entrance, he lifts the huge gargoyle knocker and lets it fall thunderously against the iron door. He hears footsteps within . . .

Cool! A horror scene! The audience is already perking up, because they needed just this sort of scene to shake them out of their doldrums.

Genre scenes are a wonderful addition to any improv show. They take scenes out of the kitchen or office, and plop them down in other times and places. And they are populated with folks who speak and move differently, who operate by different sets of rules, and who live in exotic locations.

Improv genres are a huge topic worthy of an entire book. Here we'll be looking at how to make them rich and specific by going deeper into their underlying themes.

TRAPPINGS VS. THEMES

Many times, improvised genre scenes are really weak parodies of the genre in question. For instance, a Tennessee Williams scene will consist of the players drawling with exaggerated Southern accents and talking about how hot it is. Someone will invariably be called Big Daddy or Big Mama, and that will pretty much be it. These are the *trappings* of a Williams play, but they aren't the themes. Sexuality, lost dreams, family relationships, power, and fragility are only a few of the juicy themes in Williams' work.

If we settle for the window-dressing of genres, we miss a gigantic opportunity to use the work of great artists to explore a wider range of human experience. To improvise a Williams scene and explore power and sex is so much more compelling than to stand around and drawl until someone says something funny. (And anyway—why are you trying to be funny in a Williams scene?)

It's not that the trappings aren't important—they are. The conventions of any given genre are what set it apart stylistically. The audience's understanding of genre may begin and end with the conventions, so it's very important that they be in place when we improvise. An audience probably wouldn't recognize a film noir scene without the following elements: smoking, drinking, nighttime, a seen-it-all detective, Chandler-esque language, etc. But again, those aren't the *themes* of film noir; betrayal, things not being what they seem, family relationships, bad judgment, lust, power—*those* are the heart of noir.

Don't get me wrong—the trappings are a riot. The challenge of trying to emulate the language of Dashiell Hammett or Shakespeare is half the fun of improvising, both for us and for our audiences. I'm suggesting that we can go deeper—we can try to examine the same aspects of humanity as these great writers. We'll need to be daring, to not settle for the cheap laugh, but to plunge under the superficial into the dark, deep waters of human behavior.

It's not necessary to become a genre scholar to pick up enough information to make your genre scenes better. But it *is* useful to read plays by the major playwrights, watch films, and read books on genres. Do some homework.

In addition to reading up on genres, we need to switch our mental gears out of their modern, everyday settings and into genre mode. Here are two warm-up exercises to stretch your genre vocabulary.

> *If we settle for the window-dressing of genres, we miss a gigantic opportunity to use the work of great artists to explore a wider range of human experience.*

Name Ball

Stand in a circle with your fellow players. Choose a genre and throw a space-object ball to each other as you call out names of characters who might appear in that genre. For example, if the genre is Tennessee Williams, you might call out: Brick, Gooper, Big Daddy (which are real names from Williams' plays), and then move on to Prissie, Flower, Little Ed, Aunt Florence, etc. Make up names; don't feel compelled to stick to names you know are correct. Just try to get the feel of the genre and characters. If the genre lends itself to a certain dialect, try using that while you name each other.

Image Ball

Still using the space-object ball, toss out images from the genre. For instance, for Westerns, you might call out: saloon, sheriff's office, tumbleweeds, a lone rancher working in the corral, the schoolmarm setting up the classroom for the day, etc. Let your offers range from the very cliché to the unusual. Be affected by the offers of your partners. If someone says, "A broken spur on the ground," and that makes you think of someone hiding in the blacksmith stable, then say it. As you free-associate with your partners, you will find that you quickly move from the cliché vision of the genre to something more unique.

Which brings us to the problem of genre clichés. I think we stick to clichés when we're in a hurry. If we take an extra moment to let ourselves visualize Westerns we've seen, we may be flooded with all kinds of images, not simply the cartoonish vision of the showdown at the saloon. Another limitation on our imaginations may be that when we think of genres, we think of other *improv* scenes we have seen in that genre, instead of a book, play or film from the genre. Nine times out of ten, when an improviser gets the suggestion of "Western" from the audience, the improviser will start polishing a bar. Other

At the top of genre scenes, we often think of other IMPROVISED genres we have seen, and mimic those.

improvisers will join in the saloon scene. Eventually someone will run in and say that the bad guy (often named Black Bart) is riding into town, looking for the sheriff.

Think of three Western movies you have seen. Do any of them start this way? You can vary your genre scene starts by taking that extra moment to let your creative imagination suggest a fresh image to you. Or start the scene by establishing a *relationship,* and add the trappings of the genre in as the scene unfolds.

Thematic Practice

Here's a simple way to practice genre themes. Pick a genre and have everyone brainstorm themes. As a group, decide which of the offers are truly themes, and which are merely conventions. Then, choose one theme to explore in a series of scenes all set in the same genre. For example, the group has chosen "Western," and the following suggestions are made:

- a saloon
- cattlemen vs. ranchers
- man vs. nature
- horses
- chaos vs. order
- an ex-gunfighter sheriff
- the prostitute with the heart of gold
- civilization vs. savagery
- taming the unknown
- a limping sidekick
- good vs. evil
- integrity

The group now decides that the following are merely trappings: saloon, horses, the ex-gunfighter sheriff, the prostitute, the sidekick. From the remaining themes, the group chooses to focus on civilization vs. savagery. The ensemble proceeds to do a series of short scenes, all exploring that one theme. The following stories might emerge:

- the mayor of the town beats up the prostitute in the whorehouse
- a laborer stops to help the wagon train that has broken down outside town
- two ranchers shoot a beloved horse that has broken a leg
- a young man decides to avenge the deaths of his parents, who were shot in front of him
- an Indian mother and her young daughter are captured by soldiers and assaulted
- the people of the town vote (in a meeting held in the church) to hang anyone caught stealing horses

---

Your ensemble can practice any genre this way. In a group of more than five or six people, you will probably find that among you, you possess a fair knowledge of most genres.

Westerns are one of the more straightforward genres. You may be wondering how this works for more complicated genres, like film noir. It works very well—precisely because it simplifies everyone's efforts around one major idea. Let's say your group is practicing the film noir genre, and you have picked "nothing is as it seems to be" as your theme. You might find yourself in scenes like these:

- the wife of his former partner visits the detective on the police squad. She is there to ask for help
- a slimy informant behaves in an unexpectedly courageous way (and dies protecting the detective)
- the major benefactor to the orphanage runs a white slavery ring
- a double-crossing underworld figure pulls a triple-cross on his partners and steals the jewels for himself
- an honest young newspaperman doesn't report a murder when he is threatened by the thugs who committed it

Practice brainstorming the deeper themes of genres with your ensemble.

- a priest hides a criminal
- the detective lets a criminal go free to save an innocent person's life

One of the challenges of film noir is that it's very hard to improvise a complicated mystery story. That's a skill in and of itself. After you've practiced themed genre scenes for awhile, you may find that branching out to experiment with more complicated plots feels easier. And even if you never quite achieve the goal of telling complex stories, you will still have given the audience a much more satisfying genre experience by exploring the deeper themes.

Be aware that there may be several subcategories within a single genre. For instance, the Western film genre encompasses wildly disparate examples: 1930s singing cowboy movies, spaghetti Westerns, and the films *High Noon, McCabe and Mrs. Miller,* and *Unforgiven.* Western novels include those by authors Zane Gray, Louis L'Amour, and Larry McMurtry. Each of these examines frontier life in a different way. Don't limit yourself to one idea; see how many different kinds of Westerns you can explore.

Any genre may contain several subcategories.

Genres without Suggestions

While most improvisers will get a suggestion from the audience before starting a genre scene, it's good practice to start genre scenes without suggestions, and see if your ensemble can become adept at picking up on initial genre offers. This is where trappings come in especially handy, as these visual and verbal clues help us know in what genre we are working. For instance, if my partner starts a scene using an upper crust British accent, I may deduce she is attempting to begin any one of the following types of scenes:

Practice starting scenes without naming the genre.

- Shakespeare
- Oscar Wilde
- Noel Coward
- Tom Stoppard
- Alan Ayckbourne
- Harold Pinter

I won't know which offer she is making without more information, so I will watch and listen carefully for more clues. She may be moving in a very mannered, old-fashioned way, which will help me rule out Pinter, Stoppard, and Ayckbourne. Only when I listen to the specifics of her speech will I be able to decide between Wilde and Coward, and guess what? Even then, I am likely to make a mistake! The purpose of this exercise is to help you feel less afraid to make choices about genres. Even if you're wrong—who cares? Just make a choice, boldly, and then plunge ahead with the scene.

I also enjoy starting genre scenes on stage without a suggestion. There's a school of thought that it is more fun for the audience to know what you're attempting, and I can certainly see the logic in that. I also think it's fun for the audience to see the improvisers struggling to come to an agreement about what genre they are playing. It makes genre work riskier, more exploratory.

Pay Attention to Details

People in other time periods were constrained by more than their clothing. When practicing genre scenes, spend some of your rehearsal on the small aspects of time and place, such as customs, comportment, and mores. Women in Victorian England did not have jobs, sit around the house in pants, or run easily upstairs and back. They wore yards of constraining clothing, which made hurrying impossible. Similarly, they were expected to behave in certain ways to be deemed respectable. Actors imposing modern sensibilities on other time periods can easily ruin genre scenes.

Here's a pet peeve of mine. It's easy to get cheap laughs by standing outside the genre or time period and poking fun at it. This usually comes in the form of "commenting" on the scene or making a modern reference. My least favorite example of this occurs in Shakespeare scenes. One improviser may name another "Lavoris of the Morning Breath," or something like that. And then we'll usually be treated to a speech about how bad his breath smells. Ugh. If you accidentally name a character after a household product, don't sweat it. But please avoid the urge to get laughs at the expense of the scene.

People in other time periods were constrained by more than their clothing. Spend time rehearsing the small aspects of time and place, such as customs, comportment, and mores.

One last thought about genres: exploring different times and places will likely expand your range of characters. I find that doing characters in genres helps me explore different aspects of myself, as I am working to filter my impulses and responses through someone in very different circumstances. When I'm playing a woman in another time period, I must exercise restraint and not flex my modern feminist muscles.

Men have the same challenge. Men today are often expected to be open, emotionally accessible, sensitive, and thoughtful. In times past, men were expected to be stoic, strong, aggressive, and successful. Our job as improvisers is to serve the story. If that means that a sensitive new-age improviser has to act like an ass, so be it.

Genres free us to explore behavior that would ordinarily be off-limits. By their very *otherness*, genres offer the opportunity to look at relationships, power, sex, faith, money, and death in a different way. And you thought you were just doing a Shakespeare scene!

Genres offer the opportunity to look at relationships, power, sex, faith, money, death, and OURSELVES in a different way.

Looking into the Abyss
Long Forms

"Long-form improvisation" is a blanket term that can be applied to any improv form that lasts longer than ten minutes. The category includes Harolds, triptychs, one-act or full-length plays, genre formats, and any other form, well—that lasts longer than ten minutes.

In the past thirteen years, I have performed in these types of long forms: musicals, Westerns, films noir, Jacobean tragedies, action movies and Merchant Ivory films; improvised plays in the style of Shakespeare, Tennessee Williams, Harold Pinter, David Mamet, Eugene O'Neill, Moliere; Mask shows, beach blanket movies, soap operas, documentaries, romance shows, '40s movies, triptychs, and Robert Altman-ish character studies. I've experienced the exhilaration and terror of standing in the wings without a clue what's going to happen next. By turns, I've made good contributions and bad, played memorable characters and ciphers, been ecstatic at the outcome of the story and disappointed. I have sung on key and off, shone brilliantly and sucked eggs. Happily, at the end of every show, I have taken bows with my colleagues and basked in the thunderous appreciation of the audience—which was always astonishingly enthusiastic, no matter what my opinion of the show.

The audience is always amazed that improvisers will even attempt a long-form show; succeeding is just icing on the cake.

Long-form improvisation is an advanced art. But there are a few simple ideas I'd like to share with you that can make it more accessible. In this chapter we will take a look at some basic skills to incorporate when you are exploring long-format work. For our purposes, we'll assume you are doing formats lasting at least thirty minutes.

Long forms offer the opportunity for improvisers to play the same characters for an extended period of time. We get to show the audience multiple facets of our characters—and we can be surprised by their behavior in different circumstances. We can tell longer, more complex stories, and explore ideas from more than one angle.

The difficulty with long forms is that we have to retain a lot of information (names, places, narrative, relationships) for quite awhile, and of course, new offers are constantly piling up while we are trying to keep our mental inventory current. In addition, we have to exercise restraint in the offers we add to the story, as it's easy for a long form to mushroom out of control in a matter of minutes. The following format is great for learning some basic long-form skills.

Six Degrees of Separation

This format uses six players. Here's how it's structured:

- Players A and B do a short scene (this is Scene 1).
- When Scene 1 is concluded, one of them (let's say it's Player A) leaves the stage.
- Player C joins Player B and they play a new scene (Scene 2). Player B portrays the same character as in Scene 1.
- When that scene is concluded, Player B leaves the scene.
- Player D joins Player C and they play a new scene (Scene 3). Player C is the same character as before.
- Play continues in this way until Player F has played her scene with Player E (Scene 5). Player E then

leaves the stage and Player A returns for the final scene (Scene 6). Player A is the same character as in Scene 1, and Player F is the same as in Scene 5.

When the form is finished, the audience has seen six scenes, and has seen each character in two scenes.

I've used this format to look at different aspects of human interaction, including public vs. private faces and varying status relationships. I also use it to give students practice playing well-defined characters. It's called "Six Degrees of Separation" because it explores the idea that everyone in the world is connected to each other through an average of four other people. Thus, it works best to play the scenes as if the characters don't know they have people in common. And players should avoid making any references to the previous scenes. This is difficult at first, but leads to a much richer experience for the audience, as we'll see in the example below.

Scene 1: Margie, a manicurist, is talking to her customer, Blanche, who is describing her unhappy marriage. In this scene we may see Margie in her public, cheerful mode, dispensing advice; we may see Blanche in her private mode (Blanche may also be playing low-status to Margie).

Scene 2: Blanche is picking up her ten-year-old daughter Daphne from the principal's office. Daphne has been getting into fights at school. In this scene, we may see Blanche in her high-status, public mode and Daphne in her public mode as well. It's possible that Blanche will not be acting like Mother of the Year in this scene—she may be angry and a bit out of control. Or she could be sad and defeated. Any number of choices could work, as long as we see *an emotionally different side of her* than we saw in the first scene.

One of the lovely things about this form is that the audience knows why Blanche is behaving badly (the unhappy marriage) but the people around her do not. This lends depth and poignancy to all her interactions.

Scene 3: Daphne is playing with her best friend Billy. They are exploring the world in their pirate ship, standing on the deck, looking out at the horizon. We may see Daphne at her happiest in this scene. Billy is also happy and high-spirited. The main thrust of the scene might be that these two kids are very

Long forms demand that we show multiple facets of each character.

close, and are at their most joyful when creating a world from their own imaginations.

Scene 4: Billy is saying good-bye to his next-door neighbor Frank, who has been drafted and is leaving for the war. In this scene we get to see another side of Billy, and we may see Frank in the benign high-status role of loving older friend.

Scene 5: Frank is in an army hospital in Seoul, with a nurse (Norma) taking care of him as he dies.

Scene 6: After the war, Norma comes to Frank's hometown to bring the last letter he dictated home to his mother (Margie the manicurist from Scene 1). Margie and Norma have tea and talk about everyday things to avoid the pain of talking about Frank.

Let's look at what did and didn't happen in this cycle of scenes. What did happen: 1) we saw each character in two very different circumstances, so the actors got to explore different aspects of their characters; 2) the players created very different relationships for each of the characters; 3) we saw a fine thread weaving through all these lives, even though the characters themselves were unaware of the connections; 4) we saw six scenes that were emotionally and narratively satisfying (and could have been stand-alone scenes); 5) we got to look "behind the curtain" at people's lives and see how private concerns affect public behavior.

What didn't happen: 1) the players didn't reference previous scenes in the current scene (for instance, Blanche's marriage was only mentioned in the first scene); 2) the players didn't bridge or repeat narrative (to bridge is to stall or walk in place until such time as you finally move toward your destination); 3) the actors didn't stubbornly stick to only one emotional aspect of their characters.

You can play Six Degrees with eight players, too. Any more than eight and brains start to explode.

COMMON PROBLEMS IN LONG FORMS

Improvised long forms tend to pose the same problems again and again (some of these also arise in short scenes). In this section we'll look at six of the most common difficulties and some ways to work through them.

Problem #1: Paralysis

Long forms are complex; they scare a lot of improvisers. When we're scared, we often lose our ability to see, hear, think and feel. What makes Six Degrees such a manageable introduction to long form is that it's really only a series of short scenes. And guess what? All long forms are only a series of short scenes! In fact, one of the things plaguing many long-form performances is that the players forget that *each scene must be interesting and complete in and of itself.* In many long forms, players spend half their time repeating the narrative offers from the previous scenes, or bridging to the ending of the story they thought up ten minutes ago. (You may have noticed that this is an exact description of soap operas—both real, and improvised. This is why, in my opinion, soap operas are one of the most boring improv formats, because they are anti-narrative. The point in a soap opera is to *never finish the story*—to keep the audience tuned in week after week.)

Because we're afraid of making bad offers, we may choose to repeat offers from previous scenes, rather than make a mistake. This can make any type of long form feel like a soap opera. Let's take an example: the first scene in a long form (set in the mayor's office) is about how the town is preparing for Founder's Day. The second scene, set at the Ladies' Club, is about how the town is preparing for Founder's Day. We will probably meet some new characters, but often, the narrative will basically be repeated from the first scene. This might go on until the third or fourth scene, at which time, some improviser (sensing we need new information) is likely to go crazy and make a bunch of offers that make no sense whatsoever, just to inject a little variety into the proceedings.

Problem #2: Too many offers

Now the improvisers are faced with the classic long-form dilemma: they go into intermission with Founder's Day and seven unrelated offers hanging over their heads. During intermission, everyone in the cast will be frantically going over the first half in their minds. They'll be coming up with ways to save

> *In a long form, each scene must be interesting and complete in and of itself.*

> *Early on in long forms, our tendency is to simply repeat the narrative offers from previous scenes. Instead, focus on deepening and enriching those offers.*

the show by incorporating all the offers into one cohesive conclusion. I will give you 3-to-1 odds that this will involve an explosion of some sort at the Founder's Day celebration. An explosion or a big musical number about how swell it is to live in Hooperville.

So what is the antidote to these two dilemmas? Well, there are a couple. The first is that your story should have a central protagonist, and then a lot of structural problems will be solved, because you'll know which section of the story you're exploring, and you will also know how to make all the offers revolve around the central question. The second is to remember to make each scene self-contained, even if the overall question of the play will not be answered until much later on.

If your long form has a central protagonist, you will avoid the most common problem: too many offers.

Completing transactions is a good way to make each scene memorable without answering the overall question of the story. Take *MacBeth* as an example. We know who the central character is. When we watch the famous scene with Lady MacBeth (in which she convinces her husband to murder Duncan), we are interested in the transaction before us, in their sexual relationship, in her ability to manipulate him, in his thirst for power and recognition. We want to see this transaction completed right now, in front of us. Will she succeed in convincing him? Even if she does, he won't be killing Duncan in this scene—that will happen later—and we won't know the consequences of that action until the end of the play.

Complete the transaction in each scene.

This is a great scene in and of itself. We understand that we will not know the outcome of the story for awhile, but we also understand that we are watching something captivating right now—and that the current scene is important to the final resolution of the story.

Problem #3: Remembering everybody's name

Another big problem in long forms is remembering the names of all the characters (this becomes even more complicated if each improviser is playing more than one role). One of the best ways to address this is to say names A LOT in the first few minutes after meeting a new character. This may have the feel of a Dale Carnegie training seminar, and may sound something like this: (the mayor has just been introduced to Nathaniel Wilson). The mayor says: "Well, Wilson, did you say

Say character names several times.

your name was? Well, Mr. Wilson, or may I call you Nathaniel? "Well, Nathaniel, I'm very pleased to meet you." You get the idea. Say the name again and again, not only for your own benefit, but for the benefit of your fellow players who are no doubt standing in the wings whispering madly to one another, "What was his name? Did you catch his name? What did he call him?" The more you say the name, the likelier it is that it will remain the same throughout the show.

It's also extremely handy to have someone backstage who writes down all the character names (and relationships) so you can review them at intermission.

Problem #4: Knowing where the story should go next

Let me repeat something from earlier: there is no preordained "right place" for any story to go. Any story, whether long or short, can branch off in a hundred different directions, and they could all be made to work. It is true, however, that some choices will be easier to work with than others.

There's no such thing as "The Story" existing in its entirety, in advance of the end of the show. The story exists one moment at a time, as you and your fellow players create each moment. It's like a string of pearls—each scene is a pearl, and each pearl gets threaded onto the string one at a time. That's the most important thing to remember, even if somebody wants to pretend the story had only *one* possible direction, and you blew it completely. That person is under a misimpression. If you can look at each scene separately and follow your instincts, it will take the pressure off, and you'll have a greater chance of making choices that will be easily understood by your partners.

At this point, it's worth mentioning the role the audience plays in long forms. The audience has a tremendous capacity to fill in gaps and mend broken stories. One thing I've learned from directing Six Degrees in front of audiences is that they use this capacity without even knowing it. Audiences are capable of overlooking huge leaps in logic. They are also not only able, but also happy, to follow jumps in time and space. They don't necessarily want the story to be linear; in fact, because they are relaxed and sitting in the dark, they may be far more interested in watching the story unfold layer by layer, in a non-linear fashion. Remember, too, that it's your responsibility to make each scene

There is no preordained "right place" for any story to go.

The audience has a tremendous capacity to fill in gaps and mend broken stories.

interesting in and of itself. If you're providing the audience with rich characters and multi-faceted relationships, you'll hold their attention, and a lot of other ills will be forgiven.

One of the tricky things about "where the story should go" is that we improvisers are so heavily influenced by the scene we are watching. If we're watching a scene about someone applying for a job, our knee-jerk impulse is that the next scene should be about that person on the first day of work. But who knows? Maybe the next scene should be about something completely different—about the hero having dinner with his girlfriend, or about the fact that the company is involved in illegal activities. And when we do see our hero at work, maybe it won't be his first day at all, maybe it will be after he's been there a month.

If we plow through scenes in a linear A, B, C order we may find ourselves with a ten-minute long form that we were hoping would last an hour. To avoid this, it's helpful to think about cinematic storytelling. In film, we wait for the next scene to be revealed to us. Sometimes it will be exactly the scene we were expecting, and sometimes it won't. But if the new scene appeals to our inner sense of logic. we'll probably be satisfied watching it. Even if it doesn't seem logical, we may be willing to forestall judgment until we see how it fits into the story as a whole.

Improv audiences are equally willing to forestall judgment. In fact, in my experience, they are even *more* willing than they would be at a scripted show, because they know we're just making it up as we go along, and they cut us a lot of slack.

As you're practicing long forms with your ensemble, try drilling just on scene changes. Play a short scene, and then have players either call out where the next scene might take place, or have the players start the next scene. The skill comes in looking at the current scene by itself, and making a choice about the very next scene. Try not to look too far ahead to see how it might fit with a scene that will occur in fifteen minutes. You can worry about that when you get there.

Obviously, there are some exceptions to this non-linear approach. If the current scene is setting up a big confrontation that the audience is dying to see, you don't want to slow the momentum—you want to give them the confrontation in the very next scene. It's possible to cultivate this sixth sense about

Don't plow through your story in a linear A, B, C fashion. Think of it as a movie.

momentum (see chapter 9). Play around with linear vs. non-linear scene changes, and you will begin to hone your ability to sense which would be more satisfying in a given situation.

Generally speaking, the ideas about momentum for a single scene apply to long forms, too. In the first half of a two-hour long form, the audience will be patient as new characters and new levels are added to the story. In the second half their ability (and ours) to take in new information starts to wane, and they begin hungering to see how all the pieces will fit together. So, in the second half of a long form, we should cease adding new information, and focus our energies on knitting together the threads from the first half of the show.

If you have a main story and one or two sub-stories, it's a good idea to tie up the subplots before the end of the show. The main story will not be resolved until then, but the secondary stories should be. If not, the final resolution of the story will likely be forced as you try to explain three plot points. Also, the main story (the story of the central protagonist) should have all the focus at the end of the show. The protagonist shouldn't have to share the stage equally with the lesser characters. This is in a perfect world, of course. For the most part, if you can get to the end of a long form intact, be happy for any outcome that wraps up all the story points.

In the first half of a two-hour long form, the audience will be patient as new characters and levels are added to the story. In the second half, they will be hungering to see how all the pieces fit together.

Problem #5: Too many main characters

What seems to happen most often in long forms is that after the first couple of scenes (during which a main story may have been established), improvisers who have not yet been on stage may start to worry that they won't get into the show at all if they don't make a move. This often results in people charging the stage and making completely unrelated offers, creating very strong characters, and sometimes (worst-case scenario) hogging the limelight at the expense of the story. I've noticed that in these instances, there's often a great deal more energy expended than there is when the characters and offers serve the story already in progress. That may be because ego is a powerful motivator.

This problem is best avoided by having a central hero. While it's true that long forms, perhaps even more than short scenes, need strong characters, and plenty of them, the trouble comes when the concerns of ancillary characters become more important than the concerns of our hero. We can't get into trouble if everyone on stage remembers that, and makes character choices accordingly. If you're not the protagonist, you can play a really, really sexy lounge singer, just *don't* give her a need/goal that's more compelling than the hero's goal. If your lounge singer's goals run at cross-purposes (or are otherwise connected) to the goal of the protagonist, you will be helping the story tremendously.

So it becomes clear that you can have as many strongly defined characters as you wish in a long form and still make it work. It's only essential that three or four people aren't vying for the role of hero. There's nothing uglier than a five-way hijacking.

In addition to the protagonist, you can have as many side characters as you want, just DON'T give them needs that are more compelling than the hero's.

IN CASE OF EMERGENCY, READ THIS

What if, despite everyone's best efforts and good intentions, you find yourself in the second half of a long form that's run completely amok? What should you do? At this point, I'm an advocate of simplifying, to the point of ignoring smaller, less important offers, and focusing on one or two main ideas.

Let's say you are doing a Founder's Day long form, and you have the following offers on the table:

- the mayor is in danger of losing his job
- a biker gang has invaded the town
- the Ladies' Club is experiencing infighting about their leadership
- two young lovers are defying their parents' wishes
- the kids of the town have been rehearsing a pageant
- there have been tornado warnings

Cut the dead weight. Your hot air balloon is headed for a smashup. Start throwing ballast overboard. "Ballast" is the least interesting story lines, which aren't always the ones you might think. Without any further information, let's cut the following from our example:

- the Ladies' Club
- the kids' pageant

Now, this choice assumes that those stories won't be missed, and that the audience is less invested in those characters. What if the improvisers playing the members of the Ladies' Club were a hoot, and got the biggest audience response all night? Obviously, then, we would complete their storyline and cut somewhere else. In any long form, there are always scenes that don't work and characters that don't catch fire. What if the young lovers' storyline was a dud? *Then cut the young lovers.*

But you may be asking yourself, "how can we just cut story lines that have already been established?" In the first place, you're only going to drop the weakest ones, and believe me, half the time the audience will be glad to see them go. Second, the audience will make up conclusions of their own for those stories; remember, they love to fill in the blanks, and will probably create something much better out of their imaginations than you ever could. Don't insist on dragging limp scenes back on stage.

Once you've trimmed the show of its deadwood, you can focus on the main story and any remaining subplots. Finish them crisply and with vigor, and the audience will leave the theater happy.

The worst casualties of this solution will likely be the egos of the cuttees. If you fall into the "cut" category, exit with grace, knowing that you are contributing just as surely as if you made the most brilliant offer of the night. It's always hard to accept the news that our scenes haven't succeeded, and in long forms we are given many, many opportunities to be humble. Since humility is one of the greatest skills of any improviser, embrace the opportunity to practice it. Get off the stage and don't make your partners feel bad that they saved the story.

Unlike short scenes, long forms beckon us deeper into the woods to explore characters, relationships and stories in more detail. This invitation stretches us as actors and storytellers. We can also just luxuriate in the extra time. If it's a musical, we can sing more songs. If it's a mystery, more side streets and red herrings can emerge. And with the extra space, we can simply breathe, move and risk more.

When you have too many offers, start cutting the dead weight in the second half of the show.

Notes

Improv Surgery
How to Fix a Broken Scene

You're watching an improv scene. It has started to head south: the actors have that green-around-the-gills look, the narrative has ground to a halt, or maybe everyone has been making lots of offers in a frantic attempt to get something going again. This scene needs help and you can be the one to do it.

Scene fixing is a learnable skill. And practicing it will make you a much better all-around improviser, because you'll start to understand the elements that make scenes work. The skills in this chapter are some of the same ones that will make you a good narrator or director. Here's my definition of a good director: she is a safety net for the performers—not their puppeteer. She leads from behind, like a shepherd.

Imagine the improvisers as a bunch of sheep, tooling down the road. They are happily frolicking along in the sun. The shepherd follows them from behind, with long, willowy sticks that she can use to tap them *gently* back onto the track if they stray too far for their own good. If the sheep wander off a little bit, in search of a tasty green morsel that caught their fancy, the shepherd does not whack their behinds and yell at them to get back on the road, especially if the tasty green morsel was

Imagine the improvisers are a happy bunch of sheep, moseying down the road. You are the shepherd, following them from behind and GENTLY tapping them back on track with your long, willowy sticks.

interesting to the audience, too. Narrators and directors should provide context, safety, and freedom for the performers. It's not their job to write the script or cause the improvisers to doubt their own instincts. In fact, in the best scenes, narrators are completely unnecessary. Now let's look at some scene-fixing skills.

LOOK AT THE SCENE FROM THE OUTSIDE

Have you ever noticed how much easier it is to see what's wrong with a scene when you're watching from the audience? How many times have you muttered under your breath to the improvisers on stage: "*Name him*, for God's sake!" Or "Open the letter and read it!" It's easier to spot the trouble because you are relaxed and sitting in the dark. There's no pressure on you. Have you also noticed that when you are in the spotlight, it doesn't seem quite so simple anymore? That's why it's good to first practice scene fixing from the outside.

Scene Fixing Round Robin

One player (A) is assigned to watch a round of short scenes and to help out when necessary. A scene begins, and the leader or director calls "Freeze" when the scene runs into trouble. Player A will then identify what's gone wrong with the scene. He may say "there's no clear protagonist." Player A will then address the problem either by entering the scene, or as a narrator. Use the "narrator save" sparingly. Having a narrator step in (especially when there hasn't been a narrator before) stops the flow of the scene. It's also a really tired technique, and it needs a rest. Learn to fix scenes from *inside* the story.

When it's your turn to fix scenes, look at the basic elements of story, relationship, Where, and characterizations. If you see a scene is in trouble, pick ONE thing to address, and do it. For example, let's say you're watching a scene and you determine that we need to know the relationship between the two characters. Go in as a third character and establish that relationship. If that's all that needed tweaking, leave the stage.

When you're addressing a problem, be as specific and precise with your offers as possible. Think of it as laser surgery. Be clear about what you are trying to fix before you enter the scene and address it with great clarity. The last thing the people on stage need is another murky offer. When you enter a scene, the improvisers on stage have a right to believe that you have come in with a specific purpose.

Here are some common problems to watch for:

- unclear relationships
- unclear setting
- no protagonist
- too many offers
- stalled scene
- scene needs an ending

When you go in to help a scene, be as specific and precise with your offers as possible. Think of it as laser surgery.

Below we'll look at each of these examples in turn, and I'll give you my best advice about how to remedy them.

Unclear Relationships

Go in and define the relationship as simply as possible. For instance, if you think it's parent/child, go in and make it a certainty. "Gee, Billy, your mom sure looks mad," etc. This can be done easily for any relationship you can think of. "Mr. Mayor, I think Johnson here has done a fine job of managing your campaign." "Father O'Malley, the other nuns and I . . ." You get the drift. Try to do this without adding a lot of extra narrative information. And see if you can leave again after helping.

Unclear Setting

Environments are fun to define because you can often do it non-verbally. I still remember a scene where a man was under a car fixing it, and another improviser came in and added a huge, rolling metal door, letting us know it was a gas station or garage, and not a private home. This offer helped the other characters in the scene make sense of their own offers. If two people are standing and talking in a scene and it's obvious that knowing where they are would help them, go in and define the setting, and try to do it non-verbally.

No Protagonist

To reiterate: *we need to know who the story is about*. If you can help make that clear, you will have assisted the scene enormously. Remember, the protagonist is the character who has the most at stake.

Too Many Offers

When scenes stall, improvisers often make the mistake of adding six thousand offers in an attempt to get something going again. Stalled scenes need simplification, a selecting of one offer as the most important, so everyone can rally around it and get the story back on track. As you're watching from the outside, determine which offer seemed the most important. Then go in and repeat it, amplify it, or make it more important. The other players should get the message and they will thank you later.

Stalled Scene

Scenes that start off well and get stuck are often suffering from one of the following maladies:

Wuss Disease

This is a condition where no one is being changed by the offers they receive. Usually it results from the characters refusing to be emotional. The cure for wussiness is a clear, strong offer made in such a way as to be impossible to ignore. Let's say a prisoner has just been sentenced to death, and the improviser playing the prisoner says, "Yeah, OK, so what?" You can go in as the head torturer and executioner and slowly lay out your tools of torture, playing very high status the whole time. If necessary, tie the improviser up and start torturing him.

Objective Lock

Two players are locked in a battle for their objectives, and are using the same tactics over and over again. It's best if one of the players senses this and switches tactics. If that doesn't happen, you should enter the scene and encourage them to do so. For instance, two workers in a pizza parlor have competing objectives, and they're both using *yelling* as their tactic. You can come in as the owner and tell them to keep their voices down or they'll both be fired.

Status Mirroring/Status Lock

If two characters are mirroring each other's status, enter the scene and break up the status stalemate. Endow one character with higher or lower status than the other.

Scene Needs an Ending

Some scenes hum along quite nicely until the end, where they languish and fade like the lily on the vine. Here are some of the reasons scenes don't end, and what you can do about it:

The improvisers think the scene hasn't been long enough, and are starting a new "chapter"

When this happens bring the lights down. If you're not in the light booth, find a way to "tag" the scene (using a line or a piece of business that will clearly define the ending). This could be done by using the somewhat corny, "Well, Melissa, I guess you'll think twice before going into a haunted house again." Or you might be subtler. Let's say we've just seen a scene where a political candidate has been exposed as a fraud during a national debate. The scene feels finished, but the candidate is still standing on stage, taking a dramatic moment. You could come on as the janitor carrying a broom, giving the other actor someone to share a look with. Or you could just start sweeping, indicating that his moment (and the scene) is over. Try to be as subtle as possible. And avoid a gag.

An important question was raised that hasn't been answered

You know this one—*answer the question*. Or set up one of the characters to answer it. If the scene was about a marriage proposal, and we don't know the answer, get the "proposee" to answer. If the scene was about Greek gods vs. mortals, make sure we know who won. If the scene was about a pie-eating contest, make it clear who ate the most pie. You get the picture. Just be sure to do it cleanly, quickly, and definitively.

Someone needs to change and hasn't

If you are in the scene, see if it's YOU who needs to change. (Remember: "Let someone be changed. Let it be me.") If you're not in the scene, figure out who needs to change, and then go in and help them do it. Be subtle but firm.

Some aspect of the story has not been resolved

Sometimes some small, nagging detail remains unresolved and even though the main question has been answered, this can sometimes make the scene feel not quite finished. Often it involves a secondary character or subplot. Identify what it is that we need to know, and then let us know. Quickly. Cleanly. Remember: laser surgery.

After you've mastered these basic skills, start experimenting with how subtle and varied you can be as you help scenes. Play high- and low-status characters. Help as a narrator, director, or passenger in the scene.

And now, the caveat. When improvisers get really good at helping scenes, we tend to want to help all the time, even when scenes are not in trouble. Use your power for good. Make sure your help is really needed before you offer it. You can usually tell if improvisers need help because they look like they've stopped having fun. If they're enjoying themselves while sorting out the problem, leave them alone! Audiences love watching improvisers in trouble, as long as they're having a good time. Scene fixing isn't meant to make improv scenes go smoothly and perfectly; it's meant to alleviate pain—the players' and the audience's. Be a doctor, not a control freak.

An Improvised Path
The Artist's Journey

The journey you take as an improviser isn't a straight line. The path zigs, zags, and spirals, and sometimes you may think you're moving in one direction, only to find that you're actually headed the opposite way. Improvising is like juggling your five senses, your family history, and your need to create, all at the same time. It's a lot like life. And, like life, it's often the case that we fail. And fail again. That doesn't matter. What does matter is that the failures lead to learning and that learning remains fun.

Fun-reducing factors vary from person to person, but a few culprits consistently crop up. The two most common involve the ego. Let's look at those, and then move on to some perspective-altering ideas.

SELF-CRITICISM

This is the hands-down winner in the growth-blocking sweepstakes. For the most part, I find improvisers are extremely generous and supportive of their fellow players' growth. What's surprising is how little slack we cut ourselves when it comes to our own work. I see improvisers beating themselves up for the smallest mistakes, and giving themselves no credit whatsoever for the strides, small or large, that they make. (If you're blissfully free of the self-criticism gene, you may want to skip ahead to the next sections.)

If you have a loud-mouthed inner critic, your first order of business is to picture it clearly. For years, I was taking bad advice (in art and in life) from my inner critic. Doing the following exercise was a real eye-opener for me.

Face the Critic

Picture your internal critic. If you mostly hear a disembodied voice, try to give it a shape: human, animal, mechanical—whatever seems to fit. Then name your critic. Flesh it out, clothe it (or unclothe it), see how it moves. Give your imagination free reign as you create this image. Be as specific and detailed as you can. Don't worry if your critic is someone you know in real life.

Listen to the quality of your critic's voice. Is it soft, whispering, loud, harsh, raspy? How does that voice penetrate you? Pay close attention to the words your critic uses on you. Write them down.

Now think about how you respond to this criticism. Do you follow the critic's advice? Do you avoid change to avoid criticism? Be honest with yourself.

Here's a description of my inner critic: her name is Hagatha, and she's an old, pinched-looking woman who wears a long, black dress. Her shoes are black and sensible (of course!); she wears tiny spectacles perched on the end of her nose. Her scraggly gray hair is worn in a tight little bun at the back of her head. She's pinched as a prune, and all the lines in her face point down.

Hagatha carries a huge ledger book which obscures all but her squinty little eyes. She is forever scratching, scratching in that book. She makes it a point to take notes on me all the time. Her voice is harsh and always disapproving. She's fond of talking in absolutes, "*Everyone* will hate you if you. . ." Or, "You'll *never* be any good at . . ." Her diatribes are always full of woe.

Once I started listening in a more detached way, I saw her words for what they were: excuses for me to stay safe, to avoid failure and risk. Inner critics give very bad advice. Hagatha and her gang are not interested in our change and growth; they are interested into smooshing us into little predictable boxes. They are interested in keeping their jobs.

Once you've seen your critic for what it is, how do you change the pattern of criticism? Start by learning to be objective about your work. One of the most helpful skills I've learned is how to view my work with a gentle eye.

When critiquing your work, mentally stand away from it and look at it as an entity separate from *you*. In particular, separate your personality or character from the work. You're not a bad person if you were in a bad scene. You're not a hopelessly untalented improviser just because you made a boneheaded mistake. You're not doomed to obscurity just because you can't do a Scottish accent.

Whether you talk about your work out loud, or only in your own head, start using neutral language to describe it. Here's a model that works well for me: "Hmmm. That's interesting. I had trouble sustaining my character in that scene. I wonder why . . ." This allows me to sort it out as a puzzle, instead of thinking that I am inept or incapable of learning. In the beginning, I admit that talking to myself this way was very mechanical and felt stiff. But I stuck with the language model, and now it feels perfectly natural to describe my work in neutral terms.

I believe in the value of the critique. It's important to identify what needs to be changed, and to work to change it. But that's a far cry from the sort of punishment-hungry attitude one often sees in artists.

We all have different reasons for wanting to make art. We may not even be consciously aware of our reasons; we may only know that we're drawn to express ourselves creatively, to lay our hearts open for the world to see. And for that, we ought to treat ourselves kindly. We ought to buy ourselves some ice cream on a regular basis.

RAMPAGING EGO

The flip side of a crippling inner critic is no critic at all—the rampaging ego. An out-of-control sense of superiority is just as bad as a false sense of worthlessness (and more annoying to your fellow artists.)

View your work with a gentle eye.

When critiquing your work, stand away from it and look at it as an entity separate from you. Use neutral language to describe it.

We may only know that we're drawn to express ourselves outwardly, to lay our hearts open for the world to see. And for that, we ought to buy ourselves some ice cream on a regular basis.

Of course, none of us thinks we have a rampaging ego. Here's a quick test to determine your ego state for yourself. Do you argue with most of the notes you get about your work? Do you think most notes are stupid or unhelpful? Do you generally feel that you're the best improviser on stage (or in class)? Do you wish other players were as skilled as you are? Do you get annoyed when less-talented people ruin the scenes you're in?

If you answered yes to any of these questions, you should look at your self-image and consider overhauling your attitude. I've worked with improvisers who fit this description and it's no fun. They tend to hog the stage and are unable to play as part of an ensemble.

Interestingly, the egotist and the punishment-a-holic share a personality trait: they both have low self-esteem. The self-critical player hopes to deflect others' judgment by beating everyone to the punch. The egotist hopes to deflect judgment by constructing a wall of superiority.

This issue is difficult to identify and overcome (because by nature, an ego-driven improviser has trouble seeing opportunities for self-improvement). If you think you could use some help adjusting your attitude, ask a trusted teacher, director, or fellow performer what they think. Be prepared to look honestly at your tendencies and take action to change.

THE MOVING TARGET

In trying to achieve artistic goals, we tend to give ourselves very little elbow room. Many of us set what we think is a concrete goal: "to get really good at narrative," not seeing that it's a moving target. What I've noticed in my own work is that once I get better at narrative, I move the carrot out a little further. If this were simply in the pursuit of excellence, that would be great. Unfortunately, it usually means I've given myself no credit for improving my narrative skills, and still feel that I'm starting at square one. I seldom stop to celebrate the improvement I've made, or rest for a moment at this new level of competence. Instead, I immediately begin bemoaning the fact that I can't do some *other* aspect of narrative perfectly.

All growth is incremental. Like physical growth, artistic growth happens slowly, almost imperceptibly. Unfortunately, we can't make marks on the doorjamb to see how far we've come.

So how can you measure your progress? A concrete way is to see your work on tape. You can also listen to a trusted colleague or director. But more important, start stating your goals in a way that makes sense. Instead of saying, "I want to get good at narrative," try "I want to get better at narrative." Learn to recognize and appreciate each part of the learning process:[6]

- unconscious incompetence
- conscious incompetence
- conscious competence
- unconscious competence

Let's look at each of these. *Unconscious incompetence* occurs at the beginning of learning. You don't know what you don't know, and therefore, you don't know how bad you are yet. This is blissful, like all ignorance.

The next stage, *conscious incompetence*, is the most painful. When you're conscious of your incompetence, you are all too aware of your shortcomings, and worse, very aware of how much work lies in front of you. It can seem impossible at this stage that you will ever achieve even a modicum of success. But this is the point at which you must start giving yourself credit for your growth. For it is only after you have learned some of the fundamentals that you even become aware of your shortcomings. This means that you have already attained valuable knowledge, which is the first step. This phase is often manifested as you catch yourself doing something wrong during or just after the fact. Make a note of it for the future. Each time you do a bad scene, and you can identify the reason why, rejoice! You have gained some of the tools necessary to evaluate your work.

You would think that after the experience of conscious incompetence, people would be ecstatic when they arrive at the next stage, but I'm surprised how often they're not. Time and again, I've watched students reach *conscious competence*, and that's the point at which they feel they've reached a plateau and are not improving any longer. Conscious competence is the level at which you're making choices that pay off. You know

---

[6]. The source of this model is often credited to Abraham Maslow, although some references indicate it may have originated with the 16th century Zen master Takuan.

how to add to the narrative, or succeed (through *intentional action*) at playing a well-rounded character. These choices and actions are made consciously and you're fully aware of them. During this phase, improvising will probably feel easier. This may be why consciously competent improvisers feel they've stopped growing. I think we believe that learning must always be effortful, and if we're proceeding easily, we must not be learning anything.

If you feel you're on a plateau, you've most likely reached the stage of conscious competence. You should celebrate.

When you feel like you're on a plateau, you've probably stopped struggling. This means that competence is coming more easily to you, and you're succeeding more often. Be happy! Try to think back to how you felt a few short weeks or months ago when you were "hopelessly untalented," and give yourself some credit! And, I might add, savor this phase a little bit, because from this point on, your learning will come in smaller increments, and will be even harder to measure.

After the phase of conscious competence comes *unconscious competence*. This is the bliss state, where you are no longer using your conscious mind to make choices, but are making them instinctually. This is also the point in your work where you will be surprised by your own choices, because they'll be coming from a deeper place.

Unconscious competence arrives unbidden. The more you think, or try, the less likely you will be to reach this stage. This is the phase of letting go. It involves dropping all your conscious efforts, and trusting that what you know will be expressed outwardly if you just stay out of the way. This is sometimes described as the flow, zone, or trance state. When you sense you have reached it, wallow, wallow, wallow.

Now, having divided up the stages of learning into neat little boxes, let me point out that it's seldom a smooth, balletic passage from one stage to the next. More likely, you'll be moving through the stages nicely in one area of improv while stumbling around in conscious incompetence in other aspects. Keep your wits (and sense of humor) about you.

THE ONE AND ONLY YOU

A few years ago I was in a creative quagmire. I was battering myself with a lot of criticism, convinced I would never be as good as the improvisers that I admired. I made mental lists of my shortcomings and the obstacles I faced as an artist. And then the coolest thing happened on a trip to Holland.

I was in the Van Gogh museum in Amsterdam, and was looking at some of his early sketches. Van Gogh wasn't very good at drawing, and had particular trouble drawing the human hand. There were several studies from his workbooks (which I'm sure he would have hated to have on display!). They reminded me of some of the drawings I had seen in high school art classes: the same disproportion and ungainliness. But as the sketches progressed, Van Gogh improved. He is not famous for his drawings. His genius lay in another place. But the fact that he wished he could draw, that he studied and persisted, made me feel like a fellow traveler.

And then it hit me: after Van Gogh studied traditional approaches to painting, he created his own definition of art.

If anyone had ever told me that I would have something in common with Vincent Van Gogh, I would have said they were nuts. Yet here we both were, hundreds of years apart, each struggling with our own creative inadequacies. And this realization had a great effect on me. Not only did it help me see that all artists contend with their limitations, but it encouraged me to find what is unique in myself that I can offer the world.

Too many times, I see students reaching for the wrong goal. They often try to emulate a favorite improviser, bemoaning the fact that "I will never be as good as _____." A much better goal would be to find what's unique and marvelous in their own work, and to develop that as fully as possible.

Baseline skills can't be ignored. But art doesn't move forward if everyone imitates everyone else. Just like Van Gogh, after practicing the skills others deem important, you may need to explore a whole new aspect of improvising. In a few years, people may be talking about *your* work with admiration.

LETTING THE PATH CHOOSE YOU

As I mentioned earlier, in my classes we work from goals set by each improviser. I'm all for this because it helps focus the work and gives us a specific way to look for patterns and progress. But lately I've noticed something funny happening, not only in the work of the players, but in my own as well:

Sometimes the next big leap that needs to be taken is not the one we choose for ourselves.

sometimes the next big leap that needs to be taken is not the one we choose for ourselves.

In our controlling, studied, and careful way, we try to build improv skills methodically. We choose our path and mark it out, and grow frustrated when the going gets hard. We want to manage our learning, to create it by force of will, and this usually backfires. The more we struggle and *try* to reach our goal, the more we ignore the learning that's right in front of us, and the further we are from our overall goal of becoming better improvisers.

It's not uncommon that the skill we need to learn is the opposite of the one we identify. For example, an improviser may say, "I want to learn to push the narrative ahead better, to know where the scene is going and how to get it there." In reality, that improviser may actually need to learn to listen better, stop driving, and let go of worrying about the outcome. There's an unexpected path that needs to be walked, not the conscious, carefully marked out path chosen by his intellect.

This point was driven home to me a few years ago. I had offered a specialty class called "Playing with Abandon." I was sure when I advertised it that inexperienced improvisers would sign up for it, as it was focused on how to be more committed to choices in scenes. To my great surprise, the class filled very quickly with fairly experienced improvisers—not at all the group I was expecting. In the week before the class, I started to panic, because the lesson plan I had designed for beginners wouldn't be at all appropriate for this skill level. (I should mention that I'm very proud of my ability to plan and shape a class on paper. I have a lot of my ego tied up in these skills. I'm also able to let go of a plan and wing it, based on the needs of the class once we get started, but I never go to class unprepared.)

The night before the class I sat in my office, a cold, clammy fear overtaking me as I anticipated the next day. I pictured a huge failure, my reputation ruined, my business in shambles—all because I offered a class that I didn't really know how to teach. I half-heartedly put down some ideas. These were not cohesive ideas; they didn't build from a recognizable beginning to any kind of climax. They were just some ideas for exercises.

Sunday morning dawned bright and clear. This was perhaps an omen, as we had been deluged by rain for weeks and weeks. We gathered in the studio, and I confessed my initial expectations for the class, and that I was going to do my best to offer this group something valuable. We proceeded to get to work, and the purpose of the day was fulfilled. This class didn't demand that I TEACH in my usual hands-on way. In fact, this class required a much lighter touch, as the purpose was to help the improvisers learn how to follow their instincts. All that was needed from me was that I help create a safe environment for risk, to ask some simple questions of the improvisers, and to stay out of their way as they learned what they needed to learn.

It wasn't until the class was over that I realized that I had learned what *I* needed to learn. If I'd been open to my intuition earlier in the week, I might have known why the enrollment shaped up as it did. I would have understood that experienced improvisers have a much harder time following their instincts because they have more to lose if they take a risk. I also would have had a much more pleasant time during class. As it was, I was extremely uncomfortable most of the time, feeling that I was letting the class, and myself, down. It was clear later (over a cup of hot tea) that I had set the wrong goal for myself and had chosen the wrong kind of measurement. I didn't figure this out on my own; a good friend was in the class and helped me see what had happened.

My difficulty was that I was defining myself only by my past performance as a teacher. I got caught up in my ego, which was whispering to me: "You have to give more feedback. That's what you're known for. That's the only reason people sign up for your classes. You better start talking! You're losing them!"

If I had been more willing to be a blank slate, entering the class to be written on like everyone else, the experience would have been very different, I'm sure. A year before I had written a student, Dave, about this very phenomenon, and my words boomeranged. After the Playing with Abandon class, Dave and I were discussing how difficult it is for me to not know where I'm going, and he reminded of what I had written to him on the subject:

> You are in a delightful and scary position. Scary for all the obvious reasons, delightful because you have chosen to make yourself a blank slate, and when we choose blank slatedom we open ourselves to endless possibilities. When we question what we

know, what we're good at, we have the chance for deep growth and the re-creation of our sense of self, because one of the things we can choose to wipe away is our old perception of ourselves, including our limitations. And then our creativity can flourish because we aren't playing by the old rules.

I'm very grateful to him for reminding me of my own advice—which, I might add, I was much more blithe about giving than taking!

Although improvising isn't brain surgery, growing as an improviser can make medical school look easy. We have to be willing to change our view of ourselves *as people,* not just performers. Often the learning we need to absorb is an internal shift, invisible to others. We may experience a shift of this sort and feel profoundly different, while those around us see no visible change in our work.

Some change (especially the internal kind) is extremely slow. It takes a special kind of patience and courage to move along the unexpected path. We must count on our instincts and experience for feedback.

Many years ago, whenever I would teach an intermediate improv class, I would give this "Surgeon General's Warning" to the students: "Warning! The Surgeon General has determined that improv causes people to quit their jobs, leave bad relationships, and become unwilling to lead gray, colorless lives." I was only half joking; I believe the process of improvising transforms us, and it's our willingness to be transformed that sets us apart.

Improvising is an act of faith. We have to trust a world that gets created one moment at a time. To live in that world, we believe in each other, the audience, and ourselves. And like explorers in any new world, we take with us hope, courage, and an appetite for adventure.

See you in the Outback.

Appendices

Appendix A
Ideas for Teachers

The study of improv includes all the basic elements of scripted work (save for learning lines), with the additional requirement that players bare their souls and imaginations to create the narrative! As class designer and coach, you're the person who makes that happen. The students are relying on you to establish an atmosphere full of trust, excellence and spontaneity. My own approach to class design is to structure classes with as much forethought and specificity as possible, and then give myself permission to improvise in the moment. Here are the steps I take to do that.

DETERMINE THE PURPOSE OF THE CLASS

This may seem self-evident, but you'd be surprised how many teachers start class without a sense of what they want to achieve. The qualities that will make you stand out as an improv teacher are thoughtful preparation and focused class plans that are clearly designed to support the class purpose. Are you trying to build individual performance skills, teach a particular improv theory, develop a tightly knit ensemble, or practice for a specific show? Once you've decided on your class focus, you can structure the exercises and note-giving process to support your goal.

STATE INDIVIDUAL AND CLASS GOALS

In chapter 5, I discussed the usefulness of having everyone in the class talk about their goals. This is the best way I know to start a class well and help ensure its future success. Let's look at this idea in more detail, and from the perspective of the teacher.

At the beginning of the series, sit everyone down in a circle (the circle is important—it makes everyone a peer) and ask them to answer the same question. Depending on the circumstances, I may ask one of the following questions: "What do you want to work on this session? What are you hoping to get out of this class? What scares you the most about the work in front of you? What's one of the challenges you face in this class?"

Obviously, you'll want to tailor the question to your needs. The benefits of this exercise are that it immediately starts forming an ensemble because each person is taking a small risk in front of his peers. Second, it invests the students in the class because before *you* start to talk, you're having them talk—and you're really listening to them. Third, it gets them accustomed to thinking and talking about their process with the ensemble. Lastly, it gives you valuable information about what to look for in their work and how to frame your remarks to them. (You may notice, for instance, that one person is extremely self-critical, another may be ready to take huge risks and wants a lot of input, etc.) It also lets you know if someone is hoping for something from the class that it isn't designed to provide; for instance, someone may say, "I want to work on narrative," and your class may be exclusively for character work. It's good to know if everyone's expectations align with yours (and to adjust those expectations if necessary).

After the students have responded, tell them your own goals for the class. Include your individual goal as a teacher, and the purpose of the class.

ESTABLISH A COMMON FOCUS

Establishing a common focus requires that you clearly communicate not only the goals for the class, but the ways in which you expect those goals will be achieved. This may include asking people to be punctual and ready to work when class starts, structuring each class in obvious support of the stated goal, and establishing acceptable methods of peer feedback. This sounds very stiff and intellectual, but it really doesn't have to be. You simply need to be specific about what you want and how you'll go about getting it!

Common focus is also reinforced in an unspoken way, and the teacher sets the tone. If the teacher is energized, positive and excited by the class's progress, the students will be too.

Shared language helps develop common focus; as you expand your students' improv vocabulary, you will bond them as a group. In addition to standard improv terminology, look for opportunities to develop language that's specific to *this* class. These opportunities are usually serendipitous occurrences that arise in the course of working together. (For example, "Pigs! Arrange yourselves attractively!" became a running joke in one class of mine.)

Design for Maximum Effectiveness

The atmosphere in class should feel completely different from life in the outside world. You're helping the students focus themselves on work that requires them to be present and attentive. Start each class with slow, intentional physical and vocal warm-ups, such as the ones in chapter 3 (pages 30-32). Then have people pair up for neck and shoulder massages. Next, choose an exercise that will allow the students to shift into improv mode and help them set aside whatever was going on before they arrived at class. I'm a huge fan of starting with non-verbal, physical exercises in pairs, often to instrumental music. This is the fastest, easiest way I've found to help people make the transition.

Pay attention to the way you structure your classes. Make sure each exercise builds on something that came before. This may mean that an exercise early in the class will seem odd or overly simplistic to the students; in those cases I'll say, "This exercise is the foundation for something we're going to do later." I've found that people will do almost anything if they understand that you have a plan.

Remember that what may seem like an obvious progression of ideas to you may not be so obvious to the students. Pay attention to their response to each exercise; look for evidence that the expected learning has taken place before you move on to the next activity.

After you've warmed up the class, use exercises that address the specific goals of the class, taking care to build them on one another in terms of difficulty, risk, theory, etc. For instance, if you're doing a character class, your lesson plan might be structured like this:

Character Class

- Physical warm-up (page 30-31). Very low-risk; the whole group is working simultaneously.
- Vocal warm-up (page 32). Slightly higher risk because the ego engages when we start making sounds; the whole group is working together.
- Massage in pairs (page 31). Focuses the energy; establishes personal contact and connection; this is a medium-risk trust exercise.
- Character Swap (page 34). Fun, high-energy, low-risk; introduces the character work that will follow. It's low-risk because the player isn't responsible for her own character.
- Character interactions from real life (page 34). Higher risk, as these resemble scenes; however, because there's no narrative emphasis, it's still less risky than a full-out scene. Players have the opportunity to explore their characters' inner lives, and how the characters interact with others).
- Three Stages of Life Monologues (page 124). Higher risk still, as it's a solo scene. Now there's a narrative component, even though the main emphasis is still on the character's inner life and how it's manifested in the world).
- Open scenes with side-coaching. Open scenes are scenes from nothing, without pre-set elements.

These are the highest risk of all; the players are working without a net, incorporating all the elements from the previous exercises.

Each time the class meets you must build the class from the bottom up. As your students get to know each other and become familiar with the work, you can introduce the higher-risk exercises earlier and move on to open scenes sooner. But never neglect building from a strong foundation. The transition time between the outside world and the work of the class is especially important.

Don't overstuff your lesson plan. For a three-hour class, you might do three warm-ups and three exercises, leaving fifty minutes for open scene work. In a one-hour class, you might do two warm-ups and one exercise, allowing fifteen minutes for scene work. It's better to do two exercises in depth than to do four superficially. It takes time for skills and ideas to seep into people. Leave room in your class schedule for learning to happen. Think quality, not quantity.

Tailor the work to the energy in the room and be ready to toss your whole lesson plan if it isn't working. If the idea of winging it is too scary, then create a backup plan in case your first one bombs. For example: if you had planned to work on focused, dramatic scenes, but the class is tired and lethargic, try some silly, high-energy games to change the dynamic. Or let's say you have a group that's bouncing off the walls, too fractured to connect and listen to one another. You want to keep their energy and high spirits, but help them focus. Try the Go Game (page 59) or any other group concentration game, to harness their energy and channel it into the work.

Here are some games that are just for fun; they can shoot a jolt of adrenaline into a sleepy or too-quiet class:

Bunny, Bunny

Bunny Bunny is a very silly game that releases a ton of energy and good will. Players stand in a circle. There are three "bunny positions" with corresponding hand movements:

- A center bunny puts both hands on top of her head as bunny ears
- The bunny to the right of the center bunny puts up his right hand only (as a right-sided bunny ear)
- The player to the left of the center bunny puts up his left hand only (as a left-sided bunny ear).

The head bunny (I'll explain how you start in a minute) will put both hands up as bunny ears. Her flanking partners will put up their left- and right-hand ears, and all three players say, "Bunny, bunny, bunny, bunny, BUNNY" as quickly as possible until the center bunny "throws" to someone else in the circle. (She does this by pointing her ears towards the new person.) The big, loud, "BUNNY" happens on the throw. There's no set number of times to say, "Bunny, bunny." The object is to catch someone unawares, because whoever was pointed at is now the new head bunny. The players on either side of him must quickly assume the correct positions and be ready to say, "Bunny, bunny, bunny." Players are eliminated if they put up the wrong hands, fail to put up their hands, or otherwise mess up the game.

To get started, the teacher is the head bunny; players on either side of her assume the positions, and you're off to the races.

Poison Peepers

Poison Peepers is another elimination game that's played strictly for laughs. Players sit on the floor in a circle. They all put their heads down, and while in that position, they decide if they will look straight up, to the right, or to the left. The teacher calls, "One, two, three—LOOK!" and everyone lifts their heads simultaneously.

If you're looking into the eyes of someone else, you're both eliminated. You both scream and roll out of the circle. The survivors make a smaller circle and the game is played again. Play continues until only two players remain. They are the winners.

Enemy/Defender

This is a great game to shake people out of the doldrums. Everybody plays this game simultaneously. All players are standing. Each player looks around and secretly decides who in the group is his pretend enemy (we call it the "Faux Foe") and who is his pretend defender. Once everyone has picked these two people, the teacher says, "Go," and players start moving around the room.

The object is to keep your defender between you and your enemy at all times. You may be all the way across the room from both of them, but their relative positions should be: enemy, defender, you (like planets orbiting around the sun). Keep moving as necessary to stay "safe."

Players should not run. If you're using this game with junior high or high-school students, it's sometimes useful to have them fold their arms across their chests so they don't shove each other. This is an action-packed game with lots of whooping and hollering.

After a minute or so, call out, "Freeze! Who's out of position? Raise your hands." Then, from their current positions, have everyone choose a new enemy and a new defender and play the game again.

There are no eliminations in Enemy/Defender; it's just total mayhem and movement.

The Diane Rachel Variation:

Diane Rachel put this spin on Enemy/Defender, which I like a lot. After you've played the normal way a couple of times, have the players choose someone they're defending, choose that person's enemy, and place themselves between those two parties.

This causes a huge clumping action that's very fun and intimate in a non-threatening way.

These games are also good to use if you've been doing a lot of dramatic scene work and want to lighten the mood.

Now let's look at the four main types of classes, and some exercise ideas for each.

Improving Individuals' Skills

Individual skill-building classes can be very successful and really fun to teach. Students are automatically interested in the curriculum, because it's focused on improving their work. Since the emphasis is on the individual, you don't have to worry about getting the whole class to the same skill level. You can have varying skill levels in the class and still make the work challenging and exciting to even the most skilled improviser. Also, several different improv skills can be taught in the same class, depending on each player's personal goal. This lends variety and texture to each session.

Here are two of my favorite exercises for focusing on one or two players at a time.

Spotlight Drill

Each class session, devote a set amount of time to one player's development. For example, this week Eddie is trying to work on his character range. The teacher may say, "OK, Eddie. For the next fifteen minutes you're going to do a series of quick scenes, Round Robin style, with each of the other players. In each scene, choose a character very different from the one you played in the previous scene, and also be sure to differentiate your characters from your partners'."

The class then begins the sequence of scenes, with Eddie playing different characters in each scene. The teacher side-coaches Eddie: "You're doing everything with your head and arms. Try shifting your weight in the lower half of your body." Or, "All your characters are high-status. Play low status for the next three scenes."

In this example the choice of exercise was obvious: Eddie wants to expand his character range, so you have him play lots of different characters in the space of fifteen minutes. But what if the student's goal is less obviously addressed? What if your student says, "I want to get better at helping scenes when they get into trouble"?

It's this kind of goal that allows you to be creative. For the goal stated above, I use the techniques from chapter 16. I'll have the rest of the class do several short scenes in a row, and the spotlighted player will be on deck to help as needed. As the coach, be ready to stop scenes in trouble and ask the player (let's call her Saundra) what's needed. Have Saundra name the problem, e.g., "They're in a status lock." Then have her go into the scene and make an adjustment to the status transaction. It's preferable to fix scenes from inside, but if that's not possible, Saundra could fix the scene from the outside by directing or narrating.

If you got everyone's goal at the beginning of the series or semester, you'll have ample time to come up with creative ideas for addressing those goals. Start with the simple, straightforward ones, and give yourself a few weeks to mull the more esoteric goals. Eventually you should be able to come up with a Spotlight Drill for almost any occasion.

These drills are very useful for several reasons:

- They give the spotlighted player the chance to work for an extended period of time, getting detailed, individualized feedback.
- They allow the opportunity for the other players to help a fellow player improve.
- The other players usually find that they play with great freedom and abandon because the teacher isn't paying attention to them (several of my students have had breakthroughs while helping *other* players grow).
- The teacher can focus on just one student's work and give concrete and specific suggestions for change.

I usually do one or two Spotlight Drills in each class. Over an eight-week class, everyone gets a chance to be spotlighted.

Sometimes, the easiest way to address the students' needs is to put them into pre-cast scenes. These scenes can be used to spotlight the work of two actors at a time (requiring you to split your focus and give detailed notes to both players). Or you can cast two-person scenes, and simply focus on one actor; the other player will be supporting his partner.

Cast Scenes

Set up situations for two-character scenes, assigning the players their roles. For example, in a male-female scene, one actor may be a brand-new Catholic priest (very young and inexperienced), and the woman will play a slightly tipsy, man-hungry church lady. The setting is the church hall after a big dinner. The priest and the lady are cleaning up.

When casting scenes, try to push the actors into territory that will give them the chance to practice what they most need to work on. If you have a player who always tends to be dour and negative and anti-social in scenes, cast him as a human with golden retriever qualities: happy, eager to please, attentive, changeable, etc. If your student always plays high-status and intellectual characters, have him play a painfully shy child in an unfamiliar environment.

I've found cast scenes to be extremely valuable because the pre-set situation takes the onus off the players of having to worry about narrative (the story is inherent in the set-ups) and lets them concentrate on trying something new and difficult.

The more attention you pay to your students' needs, strengths and limitations, the better cast scenes will be. I usually don't begin using cast scenes until I've seen each student play for a few weeks.

Please note: it's important that the students have the option of not performing a particular set-up. You may unknowingly set up a situation that would be unhealthy for a student. For instance, I once set up a scenario for a male student in which he was the older brother and guardian of his mentally challenged adult sister. The scene involved him explaining to her that she was going to have to live in a group home. The actor I had placed in this scenario had had a similar experience in his real life, so this wasn't a good scene for him to do.

Be sure the students know they can say, "I'd rather not do this set-up. Could I have another?" Cast scenes aren't meant to be therapy.

TEACHING IMPROV THEORY

I find this trickier than individualized training, because you have to keep moving forward whether the players have all achieved the same skill level or not. The principles of foundation building apply here, not only in each separate class session, but also in the series as a whole. In other words, you set the basic blocks in place at the first class meeting, then add to them each week. Find the balance between review of the previous week's work and introducing new work this week.

In addition to giving custom-tailored notes (see "Giving Notes"), you will also be giving notes about the theory. Students are hungry for lists of do's and don'ts; these can be a trap as students may cling to them too tightly. When improvisers become more skilled, these do's and don'ts can actually hinder their progress.

I try to avoid saying "always" or "never," and instead state theory notes in terms of their *intent*. For example, instead of saying, "always say 'Yes,'" I'll say, "Keep the story moving forward." Because that's the real purpose of the Always Say Yes rule—moving stories forward.

Whether you're teaching improv theory or a class geared to individual skills, remember that the *student* is more important than the *theory*. It's possible to become so enamored of theory that we forget we're teaching people, not philosophy. If the student isn't grasping the theory, it's your job to find a new way to frame the information so he *can* understand it.

I find analogies and imagery particularly helpful when explaining hard-to-grasp theories. For instance, the sailboat analogy (page 78) has been especially useful for describing the constant changes a character should exhibit.

Each of us learns differently. For some students, straight-ahead descriptions will work best; for others, imagery will be more powerful. For all types of learners, experience is the best way to teach an improv theory. While some learning takes place by watching others, the biggest leaps in understanding happen when the student is up and working. So keep the lecturing to a minimum and allow as much time as possible for scene work.

Here's an outline of a class to introduce the protagonist-centered narrative structure for the first time:

Narrative Class

- Physical warm-up
- Vocal call and response
- Massage
- Overview of structure (page 92). Briefly explain the five steps of the structure.
- Protagonist Round Robin (page 95). The teacher calls "Freeze" when she thinks there's a protagonist; the class says who they think it is. This introduces the concept in a low-risk way.
- Protagonist Round Robin. The teacher calls "Freeze" when she sees a protagonist; this time, only the actors point to the protagonist. Increased risk level for the actors.
- Protagonist Round Robin with multiple characters. Play is the same as before; this time, discuss what helps or hinders the clear establishment of the hero. Risk level hasn't increased, but difficulty level has.
- Short scenes, first with two people, then group scenes. Focus is on establishing the protagonist; discuss how the scenes progressed with/without central heroes. Now the students are expanding their understanding of the theory.

One significant difference between a theory class and an individualized skill class is the amount of group discussion. It's your job to monitor the overall comprehension of the students at each step in the process and expand or limit discussion as necessary. Strike a balance between the needs of the few and those of the many.

DEVELOPING ENSEMBLE

No matter what the theater project, it will be more creative and productive if you have a strong, closely knit ensemble, so don't shortchange that process. At the beginning of a time-constrained project, it can be easy to want to leap ahead to the "real work," but unless you've built a strong group foundation, the work will suffer. And ensemble can be developed simultaneously with content work.

I know from personal experience how much the group dynamic influences the success of a class. When everyone in the group is committed not only to personal exploration, but also to mutual support and risk-taking, the classes tend to be far more successful than instances where individuals are focused only on themselves. In our classes, we often found that even when the work was progressing slowly, the goodwill and common focus of the group sustained us, and eventually helped us all achieve goals we never thought possible.

This was often the case for me, especially when I was going through difficult periods in my life. A few years ago, my father died after a long struggle with Alzheimer's disease, and the years leading up to his death were very hard. During that time I was teaching a lot, and often felt ill-equipped for the task. Time and again I was struck by how much energy was generated by the students' enthusiasm, not only for their own work, but for each other's success—and mine. I believe their enthusiasm helped create success where my abilities alone would have fallen far short of the mark.

I mention these experiences because I think they point up the power of group process to achieve not only group goals, but individual ones. The power of a group dynamic is not that it forces everyone to think the same things and lose all individual perspective, but rather that it creates an atmosphere conducive to risk-taking, which enhances individual achievement.

To develop an ensemble, place your emphasis on group games, trust exercises, common language and vision.

Group Games

I'm a big fan of working in pairs or small groups, especially at the beginning of class, with everyone working at the same time. Choose exercises that are physical and experiential in nature, such as mirroring games, pairs dancing, and massage. Whole-group games such as the Go Game (page 59) are also quite useful. The following is a great four-person mirroring exercise.

Foursquare

Four players will perform this exercise with the rest of the class watching. The four players stand in a diamond shape, all facing the audience. The teacher puts on some music, and the player in front of the diamond (closest to the audience) starts moving to the music. The leader makes movements that are easy to mirror. The other three players follow the leader, who will pass off the leadership by turning to the right or the left. Let's say the leader has turned 90 degrees to his right. Now the player in the right-hand position (the audience's left-hand side) is the leader, as all the players are now facing him. He continues to lead the movement until he chooses to pass off the leadership to someone else.

Continue until all the players have had a chance to lead more than once. As the players get accustomed to the game, leadership may change quickly and may swing around the circle further than 90 degrees. For instance, the initial leader may turn to his left, then the second player may turn to his left, and now the player in the back of the diamond is in the leadership position.

Have lots of different types of music ready; that way, you'll get a variety of movement and mood.

Trust Exercises

Back-to-Back (page 62), Contact/Non-Contact (page 62), Hands On (page 63), and the Eye Connection Exercises (pages 57 to 58) are excellent non-verbal trust exercises. Classic trust exercises, like blind leading (where a sighted leader leads a blindfolded follower) build trust in terms of physical safety. I think our greatest challenge as performers is to trust one another psychologically and emotionally, so the games I suggest tend to explore those types of trust relationships.

Hot Objects (page 40) is a great trust exercise, and it's useful whether your group is new to each other, or has been working together for quite awhile.

Preparing for Performance

If your class will end in a student performance, you have a delicate balance to achieve. You will probably be working on individual skill-building or theory practice, but must also devote some time to preparing for a public performance. Here are some ideas to help you do both.

Identify the skills needed for the format you will be using in the show. For instance, in a long-form show, your players will need to know how to construct and sustain a narrative. You may choose to use the protagonist-centered structure from Chapter 9, or you may be working with a different narrative format.

Be sure to break the show down into all the different elements that will help it succeed. For example, if you're doing a short-form show the players will need to do lots of different characters over the course of the evening. If this is the case, practice quick-change character exercises to give your players the limber "character muscles" they'll need for the show. The same show may require the players to know several improv games. As you're teaching the games, look for opportunities to give tailor-made notes to each student.

Giving Notes

The greatest talent a teacher can possess is the ability to give feedback that results in new, more effective behavior. Think about the best teachers you've ever had. What qualities made them stand out from the lesser lights? My favorite teachers had these attributes in common:

- Their input was based on information I had been exposed to
- When they gave feedback, it was constructive, specific and active (meaning that it suggested what new tactic should be tried to achieve a certain goal)

- They were confident without being arrogant, receptive without being pushovers, and they encouraged questioning and experimentation

Here are my thoughts on how to achieve that ideal.

Comment First on What's Working

Initial praise helps people open up to constructive criticism. Beyond that, there's an excellent practical reason to start positive: you can then frame your new suggestion by comparing, contrasting or linking it to what's already working. For example, a student has just finished a scene in which she was laying out narrative very efficiently, but her character work was thin. Your note might be, "Elizabeth, the story elements you were adding were great. You were so focused on them, and that really showed up in how clear your offers were. Because you were so focused on the narrative, your character work got lost. This time, try to put the same energy and attention into the character that you were putting into the narrative."

Most of us can feel when we're doing something fully and well. By linking the character note to the narrative work, the teacher provides the opportunity to let the actor make the bridge between the two behaviors. You have also implied that the actor is good at narrative, and doesn't need to worry quite so much about it; it's appropriate now for her to start attending to other aspects of her improv.

Suggest Only One Change at a Time

Make your suggestion as specific and concrete as possible. When you limit your suggestions to one at a time, the actor can really focus on the suggestion, try it out, and then evaluate it. If you give too many suggestions simultaneously, it's very hard for the actor to incorporate them, and even harder to evaluate their effectiveness.

Suggest a Positive Action (Instead of Saying "Stop")

Telling someone to stop doing something is nearly useless. Figure out what the improviser should be doing instead, and state it as a positive action. For instance, instead of telling a student,

"Stop blocking," I'm more likely to say, "When Julie said you were going to be fired, you stepped backward and crossed your arms. Next time, step forward, open your arms and respond non-verbally." In this instance, I have determined that the student gets negative when his ego engages and that causes him to block; by removing his ability to speak and giving him new physical instructions, I hope to get his ego out of the way long enough for him to experience a different response in the scene.

Tailor Your Notes

I believe the best notes are custom-tailored to the individual player. In other words, I try not to give improv rules as notes; instead, my focus is on seeing what's preventing the student from moving forward, and addressing that in my notes.

I look for patterns and tendencies in peoples' work, and tailor their notes accordingly. For example, instead of saying, "Mark, you need to connect with your partners," I might say, "Mark, you have a tendency to isolate yourself onstage, physically and emotionally. In the next scene, try making yourself the protagonist (by speaking in the 'I') and make physical contact with your partners." These two adjustments will connect the player with the other actors.

Giving this kind of detailed, individualized note requires keen observation on your part, but the payoff is *huge*. The more you can tailor your notes, the greater your students' growth will be.

Let the Student Respond

When the actor has made an adjustment, give a note at the end of the scene about how it worked. If there's time, let the actor talk about any changes she noticed as a result of trying the new idea. After a scene is over, the student makes *intellectual* sense of the experience. This helps lock in the learning.

Make Yourself an Ally

When you talk with students, convey by your words, voice and body language the idea that you're standing next to the student, and together you're looking out at his work. I see improv as a fascinating puzzle and I try to embody that when I give notes. It's just a big puzzle, and I might have a piece, and the student certainly has many pieces, and together (with the rest of the class, when appropriate) we're trying to assemble it. The key is to make yourself an ally of the student, and not a critic.

If you're also a performer, it helps to reference your own experience when you give notes. This lets the student know you're a fellow-traveler. For instance, you might say, "I'm sympathetic to you, because I find physical characterizations hard, too." After saying what you have in common, you can share the techniques you've used to overcome the problem. Don't use this as an excuse to drone on and on about your own work; keep your remarks short and case-specific. I think it's easier for students to get input from someone else who's traveling on the same path as they are than to get it from someone who's sitting on a mountaintop looking down. (Also, I find it really relaxing, because I'm not trying to live up to some weird ideal of a know-it-all. It lets me make mistakes and take risks as a teacher.)

Raise the Bar

Help people exceed their own expectations by having high expectations of them yourself. The less experienced the performer, the more important this becomes. Fear and unwillingness to risk have a way of obscuring our ability to make big leaps. I acknowledge students' fears, and then try to loan them courage from the certainty of my belief that they can do more than they think they can.

Peer Feedback

From time to time it's useful to let the students give feedback to each other. I do this sparingly, for two reasons. First, it can take up an enormous amount of time. Second, the improviser is likely to get many different notes about her work, which is not as helpful as getting a set of focused notes from the teacher, one at a time. As the instructor, you are shaping the growth and progress of each player and are devoting a lot of thought to that process; students often give scattershot advice based on the last scene they saw.

Having said all that, feedback from peers is extremely valuable, because it tends to carry as much or more weight than the teacher's. Also, one of the purposes of stating each person's goal at the beginning of the class is to make every member a participant in the growth of their fellow players.

So I like to use peer feedback as a spice, rather than a main course. Here's how I incorporate it into my classes. At the end of each class, we sit in a circle. I give the players a moment to think back over the class session and give each other positive feedback about moments they appreciated, or that cracked them up, or otherwise caused a blip on their radar screens. Since everyone knows everybody else's goals, positive reinforcement coming from each other means a great deal. Also, twelve pairs of eyes see a lot more than I can, so students often comment on things I didn't even notice. The key to using this idea effectively is to set it up properly. This is a positive feedback opportunity; it shouldn't be a note session. Choose your words carefully when you set it up, and if necessary, guide it back on track while it's happening.

IT'S NOT ABOUT YOU

I've found it really useful to stay focused at all times on the students and what they need. When a class goes swimmingly, I always realize later that I didn't think about myself at all. And the inverse is also true. When a class starts to head south, it's often because I got fixated on myself and stopped paying attention to the students (this can happen if you start to panic). Of course, if a class isn't going well (which can happen for a number of reasons), it's hard *not* to be self-critical and self-conscious. What I've learned is that when a session starts to get off-track, I usually need to refocus myself on the students. So instead of saying to myself, "Man, this class is tanking. What's your problem? Why didn't you do a better job of setting up that last exercise?" I'll think, "OK. Something's not working. Let me pay attention to the student *right in front of me*, and figure out what he needs." This refocusing takes me out of my head and puts me back in the midst of the group dynamic—a much better position from which to teach. I try to use the same constructive voice and specific approach whether I'm giving notes to the students or to myself.

I love to teach improv. I love it not only for the challenges it presents to a teacher (how do you *teach* such an impalpable process?), but for the opportunities it affords us all to confront our preconceived notions. The limitations of self-image must be overcome if all of us, students and teachers, are to realize our full potential.

These are my best ideas for successful teaching. I hope they'll bear fruit for you when you're standing in front of your own class.

Appendix B
Exercise Materials

Some of the exercises in the book refer to lists to get you started in the right direction. This brief appendix includes those suggestions as well as some notes on how to coach the exercises.

SOLO OBJECTIVES (PAGE 132)

To assign the objectives, you can simply call out the task as each improviser gets up on stage. OR, the suggestions can be printed on slips of paper and each improviser can draw out a slip and perform the task. (I have a slight preference for the first method, as the audience then knows what the player is trying to accomplish, but both methods have their merits.)

- Touch the opposite walls of the room at the same time.
- Make your hair stand on end (without using your hands or arms).
- Clean up this water [*teacher spills water on floor as she gives assignment*].
- Bring your best friend into the room.

- Light this candle. [*Do not provide matches or lighters— let the player look for her own method.*]
- Get under the floor of the stage (or rehearsal room).
- Hang from the fly bar overhead.
- Feel better about yourself.
- Eat something.
- Build a fort.
- Snap this pencil in two (without using your hands or feet).
- Take a nap.

Notes:
- Some suggestions require props (pencil, candle, etc.)
- The facilitator is responsible for keeping the player safe; if an unsafe tactic is being tried, say, "We recognize that attempt. Switch to a new action."
- Let the player keep trying until he succeeds or until the process becomes unpleasant to watch. Some amount of discomfort in the player is useful, as it indicates whether his pleasure is based on success or on the act of being fully engaged in an activity. Some players will figure this out for themselves; with others, it may be necessary to point out the difference.

Two-Person Scenes with Script (page 135)

In this exercise, assign one player the first line of dialogue, and give the second player the second line. Simply recite the lines to each player.

1. "Would you like fries with that?"/"You're a lousy waiter."
2. "I love you."/"I don't care."
3. "Please sit down."/"I'm leaving."

4. "I have something to tell you."/"Nice weather we're having."
5. "I never knew I could feel this way."/"It's time to go to the electric chair."
6. "I know what you did."/"I have a present for you."
7. "I'm transferring you to the front."/"I miss my mother."

Notes:
- Both improvisers secretly decide on their objectives BEFORE getting their line assignments. (For instance, one player may choose "I want money from him," the other may be working on getting comfort.)
- Each improviser gets one of the lines in the pairs above. They will use only these lines in the scene.
- This isn't so much about line readings as it is about all the other ways we convey information: physically, emotionally, etc.

SCENES WITH ASSIGNED OBJECTIVES (PAGE 135)

For this exercise, copy the objectives from the lists below. Then cut them up into slips and put all the suggestions from Column A into one envelope, and the suggestions from Column B into another envelope. Two improvisers will get up to do a scene. One improviser chooses a slip from envelope A, the other from envelope B.

COLUMN A	COLUMN B
I want respect from her/him.	I want to humiliate her/him.
I want love from her/him.	I want to cause her/him pain.
I want sex from her/him.	I want her/him to leave the room.

I want money from
her/him.

I want her/him to
serve me.

I want her/him to
worship me.

I want her/him to
confess.

I want her/him to
comfort me.

I want her/him to
protect me.

I want her/him to
laugh.

I want her/him to
be serious.

Notes:
- The improvisers do not share their objectives with the audience or each other.
- The improvisers play the scene and may say or do whatever they wish to achieve their objectives.
- When the scene is over, have the audience guess what objectives the players were striving to achieve.

SET-UPS FOR SILENT SOLO STATUS SCENES (PAGE 154)

You can either assign these set-ups verbally, or write them on slips of paper and have each improviser take a slip to start his solo scene.

- You're a widow/widower standing at the grave of your long-time spouse.
- You're an 18-year-old draftee during the Vietnam war. You're sitting in the draft office.
- You're a young woman waiting to enter a convent (you're in the outer office of the Mother Superior.)
- You're a famous heart surgeon sitting in your own office looking over a patient's file.
- You're a psychiatric social worker taking a break in the employee's lounge of the mental hospital.

- You're a brand-new kindergarten teacher entering your classroom for the first time.
- You're a beauty pageant winner getting ready in a dressing room.
- You're an adult in your mid-30's, standing in the office of your recently deceased father. He disowned you when you were 20.
- You're a journalist waiting to meet a foreign leader. You are unfamiliar with the customs of his country.
- You're a patient in the waiting room of the dentist's office.
- You're a single executive at home in your apartment after a long day at work.
- You're the mother of a lost child. You are at the police station trying to get someone to help you.
- You're a United States senator in the dressing room of a large conference hall. You're about to give the most important speech of your career.
- You're a young child who won an essay contest and is now going to meet the President of the United States.

Index of Exercises

Animals and People, 116
Back to Back, 62
Be Changed Round Robin, 78
Bunny, Bunny, 213
Cast Scenes, 218
Character Interactions, 34
Character Swap, 34
Clown Responses, 33
Contact/Non-Contact, 62
Defining Feature Drill, 143
Develop the Scene Exercise, 103
Dueling Offers, 149
Enemy/Defender, 215
Environment Tag, 153
Eye Connection Exercise 1, 57
Eye Connection Exercise 2, 57
Eye Connection Exercise 3, 58
Face the Critic, 198
Foursquare, 222
Go Game, 59
Group Location Exercise, 151
Hands On, 63
Hot Objects, 40
Image Ball, 173
Imagination Walk, 145
Interactions from Real Life, 71
Location Round Robin, 148
Massage, 31
Moment from Life, 35
Moving Centers, 114
Mr. Bean Shiny Thing Practice, 86
Name Ball, 173
Objective Drill, 139
Orlando Monologues, 42
Physical Warm-up, 30
Poison Peepers, 214
Primal Truths, 24
Protagonist Round Robin, 95
Protagonist Round Robin- 2, 98

Python Practice, 87
Scene Fixing Round Robin, 192
Scenes Set in One Locale, 160
Scenes with Assigned Objectives, 135
Silent Scenes, 42
Six Degrees of Separation, 180
Solo Objectives, 132
Solo Space-Object Drill, 142
Solo Status Scenes, 154
Split Level Practice, 160
Spotlight Drill, 216
Stimulus/Response Exercise, 69
Subtext Ball, 74
Thematic Practice, 174
Three Stages of Life—Monologues, 124
Three Stages of Live—Scenes, 125
Torso Fighting, 68
Two-Person Silent Objectives, 134
Two-Person Scenes with Script, 135
Verbal Warm-up - Wheres, 156
Vocal Interaction, 32
Vocal Warm-up, 32

Notes